Mental health problems are afflicting more Americans today than ever before; suicide is a leading cause of death in the United States. The situation continues to deteriorate despite vast increases in expenditures and research designed to solve the problem.

In *Christian Psychiatry,* Dr. Frank B. Minirth offers a refreshing concept and an effective therapy that addresses the entire range of recognized emotional disorders. In his words, "I have attempted in this book to present an integration of sound theology with valid psychiatric knowledge into concepts known as Christian psychiatry." While *Christian Psychiatry* contains much that is of professional interest, its main concern is directed toward individual application. Whether you're a professional or paraprofessional, you'll find this a valuable resource for Christian counseling.

CHRISTIAN PSYCHIATRY

CHRISTIAN PSYCHIATRY

FRANK B. MINIRTH, M.D.
President and Founder of the Minirth-Meier Clinic

Fleming H. Revell Company
Old Tappan, New Jersey

Scripture quotations not otherwise identified are from the King James Version of the Bible.

Scripture quotations identified NIV are from the NEW INTERNATIONAL VERSION. Copyright © New York International Bible Society, 1973. Used by permission.

Scripture quotations identified NAS are from the New American Standard Bible. Copyright © THE LOCKMAN FOUNDATION 1960, 1962, 1963, 1968, 1971, 1972, 1973, 1975 and are used by permission.

Library of Congress Cataloging in Publication Data

Minirth, Frank B
    Christian psychiatry.

    Bibliography: p.
    Includes index.
    1. Psychiatry and religion. I. Title.
RC455.4.R4M56 1977   616.8′9   76-57767
ISBN 0-8007-1539-X

TO Mary Alice, who is my wife, companion, and friend. Her love and encouragement have made this book possible.

Contents

Acknowledgments

I wish to thank Ike Minirth, Olive Minirth, and Georgia Minirth Beach for a Christian heritage,

Erwin Tinker and States Skipper for their spiritual leadership,

Dr. Robert Shannon and Dr. Fred Henker for my psychiatric training,

Dr. Paul Meier, my professional associate and friend, for his encouragement,

Eileen Parmer for her help in the typing of this manuscript, and

Brenda Fuqua for her editorial assistance.

Introduction

Christian Psychiatry—does it exist? Is there such a field of thinking? Can Christianity and psychiatry coexist? I do believe there is such a philosophy. In this book, I have developed the concepts which I have chosen to simply describe as "Christian Psychiatry." Not only can the concept apply to Christians within the psychiatric profession but to Christian counselors in general. In fact, I trust the principles will help not only counselors but laymen as well.

In Christian psychiatry, the counselor is concerned with spiritual problems, whereas in other theories the spiritual aspect is often totally ignored. In Christian psychiatry, the counselor is concerned with psychological problems. He is not afraid to admit they do exist. In Christian psychiatry, the counselor is aware that physical problems may be contributing to an apparent spiritual or psychological problem. In other words, a balanced Christian counseling approach deals with the whole man, whereas other theories often neglect one if not two of these.

In Christian psychiatry, the whole foundation revolves around the Bible, whereas in secular schools of thought no foundation (final standard of authority) exists. The Bible gives the Christian counselor a foundation, stability, guidelines, and even "life."

In Christian psychiatry, the supernatural is felt to make a definite difference, whereas in secular schools it is ignored. Prayer, Bible study, and the power of the Holy Spirit within an individual are definitely more than tools or techniques. They pertain to the supernatural, to God Himself.

In Christian psychiatry, the counselor keeps a balance, whereas some secular schools lose the balance—focusing either entirely on the past or only on the present; focusing either entirely on feelings or only on behavior.

In Christian psychiatry, practical techniques are not ignored, whereas some schools of thought are so theoretical that they are not practical. Practical counseling techniques, practical ways of recognizing spiritual problems, and practical ways of recognizing psychological problems are all important.

In Christian psychiatry, valid psychiatric knowledge is felt to be important, whereas some Christian counselors choose to ignore this valuable scientific data. While a Christian counselor raises no knowledge to the level of divine truth found in the Bible, he does not treat as invalid proven scientific truth.

Thus, Christian psychiatry is unique for several reasons, and it *does* exist. It is a valid philosophy and contains concepts which I suspect will gain in popularity in the years to come.

March 1977

Since I wrote this book ten years ago, the field of Christian psychiatry has indeed increased greatly. As a result, I am pleased to see many more Christians receiving help medically, psychologically, and spiritually.

January 1987

CHRISTIAN
PSYCHIATRY

Part I

An Introduction to Christian Psychiatry

> The Lord God hath given me the
> tongue of the learned, that I should
> know how to speak a word in season
> to him that is weary . . . .
>
> ISAIAH 50:4
>
> The above words are so applicable to
> Christian counselors today. They
> were written centuries ago by the
> Prophet Isaiah and pertain to the
> Counselor of counselors—Jesus
> Christ.
>
> THE AUTHOR

1 An Overview of Christian Psychiatry

A Mr. A. dropped by our clinic a few days ago, asking to see me. He complained that everyone had forsaken him. While talking with him, it became apparent to me that Mr. A. has a gradually worsening mental problem that makes it hard for him to relate to other people. I could easily see why his wife, his children, and even his friends, eventually gave up the struggle of trying to relate to him. He also told me that, despite everyone forsaking him, a few years ago he had found Someone who never forsakes him, Jesus Christ.

This man typifies the need for the practice of Christian psychiatry, treating the whole person—physically, psychologically, and spiritually. Mr. A. has a need not only for medical help to overcome a chemical imbalance in his brain, but also for mental and behavioral help in learning how to realistically view and behave around other people. The stress of each problem has made the other worse, a not unusual situation. The fact that Mr. A. knows Jesus Christ as his personal Savior, however, can and should be an important part of his treatment.

Man's frustration in dealing with life's problems is no new phenomenon. In fact, counseling has been important to mankind since the beginning of time. Many have looked to seers and to the stars for advice. "Wise men" were consulted by kings to interpret dreams and to give them advice on matters pertaining to business, love and death. And, in relatively recent times, a type of counseling known as psychotherapy has become a profession.

Questions About Counseling From the Secular World

Because of the increased knowledge of the importance of mental health in recent years, and because of our willingness to talk about mental problems rather than hide them away in the attic, there has been an upsurge of interest in the field of counseling. Man wants to know why he and others behave as they do. The depressed person is uncomfortable and wants to know what he can do for relief. The sensuous woman is frustrated by her failure to find security. Why did she seek security by the means she chose? What was her real motivation? Is there any hope for her to find real happiness? Another person suffers from the anguish of guilt. What can he do to rid himself of this burden? Parents want to know the best way to raise their children and wonder why their adolescent is so rebellious. The adolescent sees through the facade of adults and is skeptical, but he too is confused and wants to understand himself. It is not surprising that *I'm OK–You're OK, Games People Play,* and child development books for parents have become best-sellers.

Questions About Counseling From the Christian World

We Christians are not immune to the pressures of today's hectic pace, and more and more the Christian community is becoming interested in counseling. To this end, Jay Adams's book *Competent to Counsel* points to the practical means whereby a Christian can handle his problems. Marian Nelson's *Why Christians Crack Up* is another book that has been widely read by Christian men and women in an attempt to understand their behavior and solve their particular problems.

Christians want to know *if*, in fact, they should even have problems. I was recently asked if a Christian could become a schizophrenic. What's more, Christians want to know *why* they should seek help. Some muse over the relationship between doubts concerning their salvation, anxiety, and their personality types. Christian men wonder why their illicit sexual urges are so strong. They feel frustrated and ashamed, and they ask what they can do.

These types of questions and problems are shared by many. And, really, this is to be expected.

This world of ours is moving at a tremendously rapid pace. For example, it took only 1800 years (64 B.C. to 1790) for human knowledge to double all previous knowledge accumulated through the centuries.[1] Even more than this, our knowledge had doubled again by 1900, again by 1950, again by 1960, and again by 1965.[2] Considering this explosion of knowledge, coupled with our rapid pace of living, I believe emotional problems will continue to increase. And we as Christians, sensitive to those in the world, will continue to find that we are not immune to this insidious affliction.

The Secular World Seeks a Solution

The aforementioned data is staggering, and to help meet the demands of psychological problems, new and practical psychotherapeutic techniques have been developed over the years. Although they do not claim to be Christian, some of the principles of these new approaches are somewhat Christian in essence. For example, the approach called *Reality Therapy* is based on being responsible, facing reality, and doing what is right. Also, *Transactional Analysis* stresses relating to others as a mature adult and being sensitive to the immaturity or childishness of others.

In brief, secular psychotherapy could be broken down into five schools of thought.[3]

The first of these is the school centering around the *Psychoanalytic Theory*. Sigmund Freud developed this theory in the early 1900s. It is based on the stages of development of man (oral, anal, oedipal, and latent), a structure of personality (*id, ego,* and *superego*), and a technique of solving unresolved, unconscious conflicts. This theory brought to light the impact of the dynamic unconscious on behavior. The focus is on individual introspection and the technique is "free association," whereby one discusses whatever comes to his mind. The therapist, in turn, listens, makes comments at times, and hopes to help the patient work through conflicts that originated in his infantile years. Therapy may require hundreds of hours. This school has received much criticism, especially from the religious community, because it has not emphasized personal responsibility. Also, because it does not deal with the spiritual aspect of man, it offers no effective way to deal with true guilt. Many ministers believe that most psychiatrists are of this school; however, only 10 percent of the psychiatrists in this country are psychoanalysts. [4]

The second school of thought is known as the *Interpersonal Theory* of psychology. According to this theory, man is a product of society, and his personality is determined more by social factors than by biologic ones. [5] The founders of this school had originally been friends and colleagues of Freud, but split with him over the importance of social factors. They felt that Freud had neglected the social influence on man's development. These theorists include Alfred Adler, Karen Horney, Erich Fromm, and Harry Stack Sullivan.

Alfred Adler was the first to emphasize the importance of social factors in personality development. Where Freud emphasized biological factors and inborn instincts, Adler emphasized social influences. [6] Where Freud emphasized sex, Adler again emphasized social influences. [7] Both assumed man had inherent factors that affected his destiny, but for Adler, those factors were social.[8] He felt man would even strive to place social welfare above selfish interest. Of course, in Christianity, we know this is not true without Christ.

The third school of thought centers around a practical, common-sense approach called *Reality Therapy*, developed by William Glasser. This theory is based on the value of "doing right," facing reality, and being responsible. These therapists focus on the present, not the past, and on behavior, not feelings. They help man to work out practical solutions to his problems. This theory states that all who need psychiatric treatment suffer from failing to fulfill two basic needs in life—love and self-worth. In contrast to conventional therapy they do not look for unconscious conflicts, nor do they permit the patient to excuse his behavior on the basis of unconscious conflicts. Furthermore, they do affirm the morality of behavior. They, in contrast to conventional therapy, attempt to distinguish between right and wrong. This is commendable, but at this point, a gap develops in their theory in that their definition of morality is relative. Of all the secular schools of thought this school has affected Christian counselors the most. For example, Jay Adams, who is perhaps the best known of Christian counselors, spent significant time in training with Orval Hobart Mowrer, a founder of Reality Therapy. This is evident in his writings. Also, Paul Morris who wrote *Love Therapy* included a chapter on Reality Therapy.

The fourth school of thought was originated by Eric Berne in the 1950s and 1960s. This school is known as *Transactional Analysis* or TA, and it is the most rapidly growing psychotherapeutic school of thought in our country today. This school of thought is based on three ego states in man: parent, adult, and child. These therapists state that in our transactions with others, we always relate on one of these three levels. This is a responsibility-oriented and goal-oriented therapy, and much emphasis is also placed on the importance of giving "strokes" or encouragement and recognition to others. Some therapists have combined the TA concepts with another school of thought called the Gestalt School. This combination appears to have practical application in some cases.

The founder of TA, Eric Berne, became best known to the public for his book, *Games People Play*. In this book, Berne wrote of such games as "Mine-is-better-than-yours," "Ain't-it-awful," "If-it-were-not-for-you," "Kick-me," "I'm-only-trying-to-help-you," and "Why-don't-you-yes-but."

Christians, too, play games, and the one I have observed Christians playing most often is "I'm-more-religious-than-you-are." Eric Berne also wrote about time structures and how we spend time in different ways. Berne has said that sometimes we are just involved in rituals or activities, to the exclusion of establishing intimacy with others. Here again, we Christians must stand indicted, for so often we devise elaborate rituals in our churches, thus avoiding ever becoming close to one another.

Other TA authors have emphasized what they would call "life-basic" positions. Many people have read *I'm OK— You're OK*. In this book, Thomas Harris denoted the criminal position as "I'm OK—You're not OK," the position of the depressive as "I'm not OK—You're OK," and the healthy position as "I'm OK—You're OK". These thoughts are not without merit and may sometimes be useful. Of course, the gap in the theory is that without Christ we really are not *OK*!

The fifth school of thought is known as *Behavior Modification*. These therapists stress overt behavior and conditioning responses. This school had its beginning with a Russian physiologist, Ivan Pavlov, who demonstrated a conditioned response in his famous experiments with a dog. Such men as Joseph Wolpe have continued this school of thought where emphasis is on positive reinforcement, negative reinforcement, desensitization, reciprocal inhibition, conditioned avoidance, and the concept of extinction.

Why a Non-Christian Approach Is Limited

The therapists from these secular schools of human behavior have given us much scientific information.

We have learned, for instance, that we all have certain defenses by which we handle stress. Some of these defense mechanisms are healthy and some are unhealthy. *Sublimation* can be a healthy subconscious defense mechanism when one handles anxiety by sublimating it in some productive direction, but *denial* can be an unhealthy subconscious defense mechanism whereby one fails to recognize obvious facts or implications.

We have learned, further, that social factors are definitely important in a person's psychological makeup. There is little doubt that the basic personality trend is set by age six. Such individual characteristics as being perfectionistic, dramatic, withdrawn, explosive, and passive are developed early and are largely determined by the social factors around us. Of course, this is not to say that the Lord cannot change people, but rather that their personality strengths and weaknesses are determined at an early age. Once a person accepts Christ, the Lord works both through other Christians and through His Word to strengthen the positive trends in one's personality and overcome the weaknesses.

We have also learned that psychiatry can be practical. We can help people face reality and be responsible. We can help them find practical solutions to their problems. We can help them through our scientific observation and their own insight to understand how they are relating to others, and how they may need to change in order to be more adult and mature. Through scientific studies, we have learned about the importance of behavior modification, a technique which has promoted significant improvements in *autistic* children.

While some of these approaches are very practical and helpful, they have definite limitations.

First, there is no standard of authority besides man's

logic or conscience. To be sure, man's logic is a poor standard of authority because a man can subconsciously use
logic to justify what he wishes. Neither is man's conscience
a good standard, for his conscience develops mostly during
his first five years of life from exposure to his parents and
their morals. Therefore, a man brought up by overly strict
parents would possess a rigid conscience. Conversely, a
man brought up by sociopathic parents would suffer from
an undeveloped conscience. In Proverbs 16:25, King Solomon recorded, "There is a way that seemeth right unto a
man, but the end thereof are the ways of death." In Judges
21:25, the author wrote, "In those days there was no king
in Israel: every man did that which was right in his own
eyes." It is an understatement to say that the end of this
course was less than healthy for the nation of Israel.

Secondly, the application of some of the new approaches
depends on man's own willpower. On the one hand, the
founders of these new approaches are to be commended
for forcing psychiatry to recognize that man has a free will
and is responsible for his actions, but, on the other hand,
this idea can be carried to an extreme, whereby man alone
has the capability within himself to solve all his problems.
We as Christians know that man's willpower can prove
insufficient according to Apostle Paul in Romans 7. (*See*
Romans 7:18.)

Thirdly, most of these approaches do not assume that
man is basically selfish and sinful. Thus, any approach
would be subject to conscious and subconscious attempts
by the individual to utilize the method for his own good
over the good of others.

Christians Seek a Solution—Christian Counseling

Christian counselors are also trying to help meet the demands of emotional problems. Jay Adams has encouraged
Christian counselors with the following words of Paul:

> And concerning you, my brethren, I myself also am con-
> vinced that you yourselves are full of goodness, filled with
> all knowledge, and able also to admonish one another.
>
> ROMANS 15:14 NAS

Inasmuch as so many turn to ministers for counsel (42
percent of the people who seek counsel turn to their ministers),[15] a review of the field of Christian counseling in general would be helpful at this point.

Many professionals have written about religion and
psychiatry in general.[10-27] Some have also written specifically about Christianity and psychiatry. Freud was not impressed with the benefits of religion in general nor Christianity in particular. In fact, he felt it was a "universal, ob-
sessional neurosis."[28] Jung, on the other hand, felt religion
was very important, and he wrote much in the field of
religion and psychiatry.[29] Of course, the work of William
James, *The Varieties of Religious Experience*, has become
a classic.[30] Although Adler's and Fromm's major contributions have been in this field, they apparently felt it played
an important part in man's life and psychological
makeup.[31,32] Christensen and Allison felt that religious
conversion might help to reintegrate a weakened ego, and
Pattison felt that there might be validity for the claim that
the therapist should help the patient work toward spiritual
goals.[33,34,35] In like manner, Bronner and Bergman believed there should be a positive acceptance or respect for
the patient's religious beliefs.[36,37] Meyerson has presented
us with a provocative psychoanalytic meaning of the Cross.
He feels that it is not only a symbol of Christianity and the
crucifixion, but also of love, since a person with arms out-
stretched represents tenderness, warmth, affection, and a
readiness to embrace.[38] He has further suggested that a
person terrified by love would try to destroy this symbol.
And finally, recent papers by Wilson and Nicoli (Christian
psychiatrists from Duke and Harvard respectively), have
pointed out the positive benefits of religious conversion,
citing improved impulse control, improved academic per-

formance, and improved interpersonal relationships as evidence that religious conversion may be one of the most profoundly transforming of human experiences.[39,40,41]

However, the major contributions to Christian counseling have not come from the professionals listed above (many of whom were not Christians), but from Christian counselors themselves. Gary Collins, psychologist and professor at Trinity Evangelical Divinity School, has divided Christian counselors into five main categories including the "mainstream," the evangelical pastoral counselors, the Christian professional, the theoretician-researcher, and the "popularizers." [42]

Categories of Christian Counselors

Mainstream counselors are the largest source of current training in pastoral psychology and counseling.[43] This source is the Clinical Pastoral Education (CPE) movement, a movement which is highly organized and which has done much commendable work with counseling curricula in hospitals and seminaries. However, many are skeptical of the movement because it is too liberal ánd some in the movement put human experience and psychology above the Word of God.[44] Anton Boiser was one of the founders of the CPE movement. Other familiar names involved in CPE are Seward Hiltner, Edward Thornton and Russell Dicks.

The second category is the *Evangelical Pastoral* counselors, a group which is made up, obviously, of evangelical ministers. They stand in opposition to the "mainstream"; and their most vocal spokesman, Jay Adams, has gone to the point of reflecting a critical attitude toward objective, sound data in the field of psychology. Even though Jay Adams is defensive in certain areas, he has reminded Christian counselors of the profound importance of the Word of God.

The third category is the *Christian Professional*. These men are Christians who have professional training in psychiatry or psychology. Many (Narramore, Dobson,

Meier, Collins, Mallory, and Hyder) are best known for their writings. Although the books of the authors mentioned above reflect a dominant belief in the final standard of authority of God's Word, many other Christian professionals have relied too heavily upon psychology and not enough upon God's Word.

The fourth category is the *Theoretician-Researcher*. These men have studied and researched the field of theology and psychology as they have attempted to provide an apologetic to face the antichristian challenge. Collins pointed out in his paper that Freud (psychoanalytic approach), Skinner (behaviorist), Rogers (humanistic), have all attacked the very basis of Christianity. The theoretician-researchers feel that Christian counselors should be able to give biblical answers. They also feel scientific data is of much importance when dealing with non-Christians.

The last category is comprised of the *Evangelical Popularizers*. These men usually have little professional training in psychology. However, they have significant insights into helping people in a practical, scriptural way and have become well-known across the country. The most popular of these men include Bill Gothard, Keith Miller, and Tim LaHaye.

As can be seen from the above categories, Christian counseling includes several fields: ministers, psychologists, psychiatrists, and related fields. Each needs the other. The minister has the biblical expertise that the others often do not have. The psychologist has the tools for objective evaluations, and the social worker often has special expertise in interpersonal relations. Often, they can greatly benefit a patient by working as a team, whether simultaneously or by referral from one to the other.

The Uniqueness of Christian Counseling

Christian counseling could be defined as the ministry of one individual seeking to help another individual recognize, understand, and solve his own problems in accordance with the Word of God.[45] The emphasis in the above definitions is on only two individuals—the patient and the therapist. Strictly speaking, this emphasis is valid, yet Christian counseling has even further implications. The entire body of Christ in a local area has a responsibility to minister to the emotional needs of one of its members, and the counselor will do well to take advantage in therapy of the tremendous rehabilitative resources (fellowship and spiritual encouragement) available in a local church.

Regardless of whether one thinks of the entire local church or the one-to-one relationship when Christian counseling is mentioned, and regardless of whether the Christian counselor is a minister, psychologist, psychiatrist, or social worker, certain principles make Christian counseling unique.

First, it accepts the Bible as the final standard of authority. As a result, Christians are not left to explore and dissect through the myriads of philosophies and their own logic, and to happen then, by one chance in a million, to hit upon a correct system of right and wrong.

What's more, Christians do not have to depend upon their own consciences to direct their behavior. They may rely upon the Word of God. If one's conscience agrees with the Word of God, then the conscience is valid; if not, the conscience is invalid. For example, in some cultures, a man might feel guilty for seeing his wife in the nude. Should such a man be told to live up to his conscience? His conscience is too strict and should be reeducated according to the Word of God. As mentioned above, in other cases, an individual may have too little conscience because of poor identity-figures and thus may have developed the attitude that society and others are bad, and whatever he does to them is all right. This kind of child develops the feeling that he is OK but others are not OK. In contrast to the former example, this is a case of a too weak conscience which also needs reeducating according to the Word of God.

Thus, Christian counseling offers not only practical guidelines through the Bible, but it points to one final standard of authority—the Bible. All schools of thought in psychiatry need a foundation and framework from which to build. The Bible is ours.

However, it differs from other schools of thought in that we dare say that the Bible is the very Word of God. We feel that it is *the* standard; thus, we can be *certain* that certain things are wrong (sinful) or right. The Bible is not afraid to call a spade a spade or a sin a sin. The Reality Therapy school has made one of its major premises "do right." But its definition of right is rather vague and nebulous. Our definition of right is based on the Bible. However, the Bible is not primarily a book of rules on rights and wrongs. It is meant to give guidelines, spiritual nourishment, and "life." The Lord Jesus Christ expressed this concept well when He stated, ". . . The words that I speak unto you, they are spirit, and they are life" (John 6:63).

Not only does the Bible give Christian counselors a framework, it gives the best framework. It not only gives insights into human behavior, it puts everything into proper perspective. It tells who man is, where man came from, the purpose of man, and the nature of man. By coupling this tremendous foundation with scientific facts and observations of psychiatry, the Christian counselor has a good vantage point from which to help individuals solve problems.

Secondly, Christian counseling is unique because it depends not only on man's willpower to be responsible, but also on God's enabling, indwelling power of the Holy Spirit to conquer man's problems. I do not wish to imply that man has no responsibility for his actions, for he does; and many Christians choose to act irresponsibly. However, our willingness and attempts to be responsible must be coupled with God's power. Through God's power, man need no longer be a slave to a weak will, his past environment, or social situations. Problems do not **disappear** when one accepts Christ, but there is a new power to deal with them.

Thirdly, Christian counseling is unique because even though man does have a basic selfish component, he, if a Christian, has a much stronger godly component. In Romans 7:23, Paul gave the description of an internal battle in an individual not unsimilar to Freud's description of the *id*, *ego*, and *superego*. The description was that of a good law in the individual mind waging war against an evil law in its "members." As a result, the will was overpowered by the evil law, and only through the Spirit of Christ was victory obtained. Also, only through the Spirit of Christ can real spiritual insights be obtained. Apostle Paul stated, "But the natural man [interpreted "psychological man" from the Greek], receiveth not the things of the Spirit of God: for they are foolishness unto him: neither can he know them, because they are spiritually discerned" (1 Corinthians 2:14).

Fourthly, Christian counseling is unique in that it offers an effective way to deal with the past as well as the present. Some of the older schools of thought deal almost exclusively with the past, while some of the newer schools of thought in psychiatry deal mostly with the present. Christian counselors can deal with both. The following two verses point to only a couple of ways that can be tremendously effective in dealing with past guilt or worries: "If we confess our sins, He is faithful and righteous to forgive us our sins and to cleanse us from all unrighteousness" (1 John 1:9 NAS); and " ... one thing I do: forgetting what *lies* behind and reaching forward to what *lies* ahead. I press on ... " (Philippians 3:13–14 NAS). Of course, the counselor cannot always expect a patient to get well by simply pointing out these verses; he must work with each person individually as he helps the person gain insight and victory over his problems.

The fifth reason Christian counseling is unique is that it is based on God's love. Apostle John stated, "In this is love, not that we loved God but that He loved us and sent His Son to be the propitiation for our sins" (1 John 4:10 NAS). Because God loved us, and His love flows through us, we love others and feel a responsibility toward them. Again, Apostle John states, " . . . whoever loves the Father loves the *child* born of Him" (1 John 5:1 NAS). The Christian counselor feels a spiritual relationship with other Christians and hopes to help them grow in Christ as they solve their problems. The Christian counselor hopes the non-Christian accepts the Lord. Christ died for this individual, and his first step to finding real inner peace is through knowing Christ.

The sixth reason Christian counseling is unique is that it is universal. It can apply to all people regardless of genetic, social, educational, or cultural background. No other school of counseling dares make this comment. The psychoanalytic school, the transactional analysts, the reality therapists, all recognize that there are certain types of people they can help better than others. Christ claimed He could help all who would turn to Him (*See* Matthew 11:28; John 6:37). Of course, this does not mean that Christian counselors can help all people, but that Christ forms the foundation of their counseling, and He can help all who are willing to turn to Him.

The last reason Christian counseling is unique is that it deals with the whole person. The Christian counselor knows that the physical, psychological, and spiritual aspects of man are all intricately related, and that when one aspect is affected, the other two are also. For example, an ulcer may start on a physical level. Some individuals have a defect in their stomach lining and are thus predisposed to ulcers. Perhaps because of detrimental defense mechanisms (a psychological factor) laid down in early life, the individual is prone to be a very serious-minded person and more concerned than most over his problems. When he carries this intensity to despair, or to exploding and hitting his wife, the problem has become spiritual. On the other hand, perhaps the individual was beaten during the early months of life. He was a battered child, and infantile conflicts were laid down that later could cause ulcers. The problem started on a psychological basis, but the physical level was affected.

Perhaps the problem did not start on a physical or psychological level, but on a spiritual level. For example, the individual may have chosen to sin and commit adultery. His guilt feelings may lead to anxiety and then to an ulcer.

In summary, man is very intricate in his makeup, and usually when one aspect of man is affected, so are the other parts.

I do take issue with those who either deny the spiritual aspect or deny the psychological aspect. I would wonder whether they are just ignorant or using some detrimental defense mechanism to lie to themselves. I wonder how some can deny that psychological problems exist when we have the objective data available today. For example, children deprived of love in the first few weeks of life will develop severe depression and may even die. Is this a spiritual problem at this age? I can understand a little better how an unregenerate man can deny the spiritual aspect (*see* 1 Corinthians 2:14), although this, too, is an unfortunate and tragic error.

Not treating the whole man is tragic because of the limitations the counselor imposes upon himself when he denies the reality of the other dimensions of man. For example, can one imagine treating a diabetic with spiritual exhortation? In like manner, treating a person with biochemical depression with spiritual exhortation alone can result in much anguish for the counselee. And how

could one treat *anaclitic depression* (a psychological problem) in a baby with a spiritual approach alone? Finally,
how can a counselor treat a spiritual problem if he uses
only psychological and physical therapies? *Man is a whole,
composed of more than one part, and he must be treated as
such.*

The implications of the above statement will be developed throughout this book, but the following brief
summary may be of help at this point.

To determine whether a problem started on a physical,
psychological, or spiritual level, each level should be
evaluated. A counselee with any evidence of a physical
problem should be referred to a physician for a complete
physical evaluation. A check into the spiritual aspect
should also be done and include such questions as: Does
the patient need to know Christ? Is he spiritually immature
and in need of growing in Christ? Would he thus benefit
from a plan for Scripture memory or Bible study? Is there a
specific sin he needs to face? Finally, in some cases, initial
attention should be given to the psychological aspect. For
example, does the counselee have a *neurosis* (cannot function adequately biologically or socially), a *psychosis* (a loss
of contact with reality), a *psychophysiologic disorder*
(ulcer, colitis, etc.), or a personality disorder? In the above
cases, a medical doctor and a minister may need to work
together.

Again, the parts are integrally related and the counselor
needs to recognize and deal with all three parts and their
interrelations. *Man is a whole and must be dealt with as
such.*

The Balance Needed in Christian Counseling

Just as balance is the key to both spiritual and emotional
maturity, so is balance the key to successful Christian
counseling. For example, Jesus Christ Himself had tremendous balance. He knew when to be directive and

when to help others gain insight through parables (*see* John 2). He knew when to focus on the present without excluding the past (*see* John 4). He knew when to focus on the spiritual aspect of man but not neglect the physical and psychological aspects (*see* John 5).

Apostle Paul also had emotional and spiritual balance and reflected this in his counseling. In 1 Thessalonians 5:14, Paul recorded the balance that is needed in counseling. I first noted this verse while I was in my residency training in psychiatry. As I was studying one day and attempting to integrate my newly found psychiatric knowledge with Scripture, my eyes fell on this verse:

> And we urge you, brethren, admonish the unruly, encourage the faint hearted, help the weak, be patient with all men.
> 1 THESSALONIANS 5:14

As I read the verse, I noted how everyone was not counseled in the same manner. Some were admonished, or in present day terminology, they were treated with a matter-of-fact approach. Some were encouraged, an approach which made me think of a psychiatric approach known as "active friendliness." And yet, others were to be helped in a supportive, friendly manner. *All* were to be treated with patience.

Thus, psychiatrically and biblically, I was convinced that everyone should not be counseled in the same way. I knew that, at times, a counselor should be confronting, at other times not. I knew an active friendly approach would help some individuals, while others would only become worse with this approach. In short, again, I was impressed that one type of counseling would not work with all men. However, only recently did I learn what I needed to know to give this thought the real impetus it needed. A student of theology shared some very interesting insights with me concerning the meaning of the Greek words in 1 Thessalonians 5:14. [46] These insights plus additional research proved extremely helpful. [47]

Aspects of Biblical Counseling

There are five variations of biblical verbs on counseling. They are: *parakaleo, noutheteo, parmutheomai, antechomai,* and *makrothumeo.*

These five Greek verbs are used in 1 Thessalonians 5:14 mentioned above. The first is *parakaleo.* Paul used this counseling verb himself as he began his statement on the different types of counseling. It means to beseech or exhort, encourage or comfort. It is used in a milder sense than the next verb which means to admonish. In the original Greek text, this next verb is found in Romans 12:1, 2 Corinthians 1:4, and Romans 15:30 quoted respectively below:

> I beseech you therefore, brethren, by the mercies of God, that ye present your bodies a living sacrifice, holy, acceptable unto God, which is your reasonable service.
>
> ROMANS 12:1

> Who comforteth us in all our tribulation, that we may be able to comfort them which are in any trouble, by the comfort wherewith we ourselves are comforted of God.
>
> 2 CORINTHIANS 1:4

> Now I beseech you, brethren, for the Lord Jesus Christ's sake, and for the love of the Spirit, that ye strive together with me in your prayers to God for me.
>
> ROMANS 15:30

It is an active verb. It is the verb on which Paul Morris bases his counseling known as "Love Therapy."

The next Greek verb is *noutheteo.* This verb can be used in a broad context in counseling, but in the New Testament it usually means to put in mind, to warn, and to confront. It is intended to produce a change in life-style. One especially admonishes the unruly, the undisciplined, or the impulsive, but we also admonish one another. It is found in the verses quoted respectively below:

And concerning you, my brethren, I myself also am convinced that you yourselves are full of goodness, filled with all knowledge, and able also to admonish one another.

ROMANS 15:14 NAS

I am not writing this to shame you, but to warn you, as my dear children.

1 CORINTHIANS 4:14 NIV

Let the word of Christ richly dwell within you; with all wisdom teaching and admonishing one another with psalms *and* hymns *and* spiritual songs, singing with thankfulness in your hearts to God.

1 COLOSSIANS 3:16 NAS

It is also an active verb. It is the verb on which Jay Adams bases his Nouthetic Counseling.

The third counseling verb is *parmutheomai*. It means to cheer up, to encourage. One encourages the fainthearted or discouraged. It is found in the original Greek text as follows:

Just as you know how we *were* exhorting and encouraging and imploring each one of you as a father *would* his own children.

1 THESSALONIANS 2:11 NAS

The fourth counseling verb is *antechomai*. It means to cling to, to hold fast, to take an interest in, to hold up spiritually or emotionally. It is a passive verb.

The fifth Greek verb is *makrothumeo*. It means to be patient or to have patience. It is found in Matthew 18:26, Matthew 18:29, James 5:7, and Hebrews 6:15. It is also a passive verb.

Thus, there is not just one biblical verb on counseling, but there are several, a fact which proves that a person needs balance in his counseling approach.

Christian counseling is *unique* in its ability to provide this balance.

I do not frustrate the grace of God: for
if righteousness come by the law,
then Christ is dead in vain.

GALATIANS 2:21

2 The Basis of Christian Counseling— Grace or a Double-Bind Message

The Damage of a Double-Bind Message

Untold psychological damage is done when an individual feels he is accepted by ones that are close to him on a conditional basis. This may be expressed in a contradictory message, such as verbally relating, "I love you," but in actions relating, "If you want me to love you, you must. . . ."

Similar to a contradictory message, but even more damaging is a message known as a *double-bind*. This message produces a paradox that makes choice impossible. With a double-bind message a child is asked to do two conflicting things. He may be verbally asked to be good but the covert message is to "act out." If the child is bad, he violates the verbal message asking him to be good. However, if he is good, he violates the covert message asking him to "act out." He cannot win. Whichever decision he makes, he loses.

Although a double-bind message such as the one above can be very detrimental to a child and even contributes to loss of contact with reality known as *schizophrenia,* an even more serious *double-bind* message is given from many pulpits every Sunday. When a minister asks someone

39

to do something for the grace of God, he has just given the
individual an impossible choice. By definition, grace is
God's unmerited favor. It cannot be earned, for this would
contradict the definition. Thus, if the individual chooses
grace, he cannot do anything for it. Yet, the minister has
told him something he must do. The individual cannot win
under this system. He is under a *double-bind* message.

An understanding of the concept of grace is basic to the
prevention of a double-bind message's being given from a
pulpit. What follows is a development of that concept, a
concept that is basic to both the Bible and psychiatry.

Grace and the Church

Grace is a concept which so easily escapes us. Indeed, it
is a concept foreign to the way of life of most humans and
thus hard to appreciate. Because of our psychological
makeup, man through the centuries has repeatedly gravi-
tated from the concept of grace to that of law.[1]

Men like Martin Luther stand as stalwarts in Christian
history as men who once again discovered the marvelous
meaning of grace. After years of striving in vain to be righteous, and after years of psychological pain, Martin Luther
found a solution for the basic guilt common to man. This
was the beginning of the Protestant Reformation, and the
world had little known such widespread joy since the early
Church.

How the Church views grace has widespread implications. A misconception in one direction results in depression, while a misconception in another direction results in
a license to sin. Where do most churches today stand on the
issue? A misconception of the term "grace" not only carries
widespread spiritual implications, but also psychological
harm.

How to Raise Healthy Children—A Comparison

God gave us the example of how to produce healthy
children when he chose that the foundation of a relation-

ship between two individuals should be based on the concept of grace. Grace implies that the love of God is free and unmerited. Just as parents usually accept their children and will have an innate love for them regardless of what they do, so God loves us. Although God does not always like our behavior, just as parents do not always like their children's behavior, there is a great difference between not accepting someone's behavior and not accepting him. Children still feel loved if parents do not accept their irresponsible behavior, but they feel rejected and discouraged if they feel that they themselves are rejected. This type of rejection leads to discouragement, neurosis, and even psychosis. Likewise, Christians may become discouraged, neurotic, or even psychotic if they feel their receiving or keeping Christ is conditional.

The Trend Today

There seems to be a trend among evangelical Christians today away from the unconditional love of Christ. God's system of grace has been mongrelized into a *grace-plus-merit* system. Consequently, rather than receiving Christ and giving of ourselves as a result, I hear Christian workers encouraging others to merely give their lives to Christ. God has already condemned the old sin, nature, and made atonement on the Cross. He does not want one to *give* but to *receive*. Evangelical sermons often put the emphasis on what one is to *do*—commitments, public confessions, restitution, etc., rather than on the big deed that Christ accomplished on the Cross.

Grace Versus Debt, Works, Law

Grace is set in contrast to debt, works, and law in Scripture.[2] *The American College Dictionary* defines these terms in some of the important details listed below.[3] In Romans 4:4 grace is set in contrast with debt. Debt implies that one owes another and must pay or perform for that debt. It implies an obligation. Theologically, it implies that an offense has been committed and requires reparation. In leading others to Christ, an emphasis on a performance of some kind, an obligation, or reparation is an emphasis on debt which God sets in contrast to grace.

Secondly, grace is set in contrast to works in Romans 11:6. Work refers to the result of labor or activity. It refers to a deed or a performance. Theologically, it refers to an act of obedience. Work refers to obtaining something by effort. A synonym for work is "toil" which is wearying and exhausting. Thus, in leading others to Christ, an emphasis on an action in response to obedience, on exertion that takes much willpower and is exhausting, or any other labor, is an emphasis on works which is in contrast to God's concept of grace (*see* Ephesians 2:8, 9; Titus 3:5).

Thirdly, grace is set in contrast to law in Galatians 5:4 and in John 1:17. A law implies a regulation that should be kept. I have heard Christian workers say, "I like to tell someone about the Christian life before he becomes a Christian, so he will know what to expect." Their aim is to obtain from the person a resolution to live the Christian life. However, a Christian worker putting emphasis on resolutions is in contrast with God and His emphasis on grace.

The power to live the Christian life is given by the indwelling power of the Holy Spirit that comes at the time one believes in Christ. Without this power, all actions are based on *willpower* (human) which God condemns (*see* John 1:13). God gives grace to a non-Christian to understand the plan of God in salvation and then to accept Christ, resulting in a change of attitude about himself, sin, and Christ; but beyond this, the Holy Spirit must produce results.

We evangelical Christians consent to the concept of grace versus law. However, we too, if not careful, will be prone to a tendency to progress from grace to a mixed *grace-merit* system. This results because the idea of grace as unmerited favor is largely foreign to our society and also to our way of thinking.

A Psychiatric Example—The Unpardonable Sin

An endless frustration or perhaps, even worse, a temporary soothing of the conscience is produced by a *grace-plus-merit* system. I recently had a patient who illustrated this principle well. This patient was a college girl with whom I had been working for two to three weeks with little progress. She had been admitted to the hospital for an overdose of sedative pills which she had taken because of depression. I had been trying to gain rapport and encourage her to talk. I had largely failed, and she remained inwardly angry and hostile. She admitted there was something about which she was unwilling to talk and had given me some insight into her problem on the night of her admission to the hospital. She asked me if a person had to walk to the front of the church to be saved. I assured her then that one did not. She stated that she agreed with me, but that she knew many people who would disagree with the view that a person need do nothing more than accept Jesus Christ as his Savior to establish the right relationship with God. I wondered if I had moved too fast with advice, rather than initially being a good listener. Therapy then progressed slowly after her admission to the hospital until one session three weeks later. I detected the patient had some things on her conscience she really needed to share. I thus began to ask her questions that would enable her to share her stressful burden.

I asked, "When did it occur?"

She stated, "At the age of sixteen." She later explained that what she had done would make others think she was terrible, and that it was the most horrible thing anyone could do. Finally, I confined the problem to an issue between her and God. She felt she had committed the unpardonable sin.

I asked, "What do you think the unpardonable sin is? Individuals think differently. What do you think it is?"

I then proceeded to share with her some thoughts others have had about the unpardonable sin (*see* Mark 3:28, Matthew 12:31, and Luke 12:10). An unpardonable sin would be the rejection of the Holy Spirit for the last time after which a person would never be convicted again. Of course, after death, grace would no longer be offered, and the sin of unbelief would no longer be pardonable. I shared with her that the very fact that she wanted to know Christ meant that she had not committed the unpardonable sin.

The other concept of an unpardonable sin would be equating the Holy Spirit with evil, and this would be a matter of the heart, as when the scribes stated Christ performed his miracles by the power of Satan.

She thought there was still perhaps another way she had committed the unpardonable sin, and that was by attending a worship service of the devil with a friend of hers who claimed to be a witch. I shared with her the thought that I could not recall one verse of Scripture that would deem this unpardonable.

Another proof that she had not committed the unpardonable sin would be if she were a Christian. However, she was unsure at this point, and I asked, "Have you ever invited Christ into your life?"

She answered, "Yes, many times."

Later, I had the opportunity to read a note she had written as a rather young girl which read something like this: "My friends ask me if I am a Christian. I answer 'yes', but to me my being a Christian is different from *their* being Christians. To me being a Christian is between me and Christ, but to them, it is between them and other people. To them, being a Christian is telling other people, but to me it is telling Christ . . . ."

I was impressed with the depth and spiritual wisdom of

her thinking as a little child. Apparently, she had become a Christian at an early age, but then with further exposure to the *grace-plus-merit* system, combined with her own *obsessive-compulsive* personality trends, she succumbed to guilt and frustration.

She stated, "I am going to hell. I just know it."

I asked, "How do you know it?"

She answered, "Because I have not done enough right."

I asked, "Do you know what God thinks of our righteousness? He thinks 'our righteousnesses are as filthy rags . . .' (*see* Isaiah 64:6). So do you know what we get if we try to get to heaven by the *right* things we do? We get a debt rather than heaven."

I then asked her to visualize Christ on the Cross, to visualize all her sins, to then visualize each sin driving a spike into His hand, and finally to visualize carrying all her guilt up to the Cross and giving it to Christ. She had an anguished demeanor.

I asked, "Can you visualize what I have said?"

"Yes," was the answer.

I proceeded, "Visualize Christ standing at your heart's door and knocking, and then visualize yourself opening the door and asking Him to come into your life."

I then shared John 6:37: "All that the Father giveth me shall come to me; and him that cometh to me, I will in no wise cast out."

I repeated the quote and then shared Ephesians 2:8–9: "For by grace are ye saved through faith; and that not of yourselves: it is the gift of God: Not of works, lest any man should boast."

I repeated this also and stated, "Nothing to boast about. If I could do something, I could boast; but I can't."

Soon a serene, peaceful look came over the patient's face. "Is the guilt gone?" I asked.

"Yes," was the response.

The patient then slowly began to improve despite her

problems. Although this patient would not instantly be free of psychological problems, I was glad I had the opportunity to introduce her to grace.

I shared with her that what we *do* and *don't do* in the Christian life is not based on a brownie point system, but on a love for Christ and a respect for His wisdom. He is so much wiser than we, that we would be foolish not to follow his leading. In Isaiah 55:8-9, God recorded, "For my thoughts are not your thoughts, neither are your ways my ways, saith the Lord. For as the heavens are higher than the earth, so are my ways higher than your ways, and my thoughts than your thoughts." Jeremiah 29:11 reflects God's general attitude when he said to Israel, "For I know the thoughts that I think toward you, saith the Lord, thoughts of peace, and not of evil, to give you an expected end."

The Simplicity of Christ and a Different Gospel

In 2 Corinthians 11:3-4, Apostle Paul referred to the fear he had that the Corinthians might be led astray from the simplicity and purity of devotion to Christ, and that they might be corrupted with another (different) gospel. The idea of another gospel is again mentioned in Galatians. The gospel is very simply the good news that Jesus Christ the Son of God died on the Cross in payment for man's sins, and that He not only died but rose from the grave after three days and had victory over sin and death. This is payment in full to God and nothing one can do can add to this. This is grace. Others have written excellent in-depth books on the subject, and just the general concepts of grace will be reviewed here. [4-11]

Grace says, "Believe only."
Law says, "Believe plus do something."

Grace says, "Everything has been accomplished for your salvation; now only receive."

Law says, "You must do in order to receive."

Grace says, "All has been accomplished; now rest."
Law says, "You owe a debt."

Grace says, "Receive Christ as Savior, and then do."
Grace says, "Salvation is based on Christ's merit and our believing."
Law says, "Salvation is based, at least to some degree, on human merit."

Law requires various works for salvation: a good life, dedication, vows, resolutions, commitments, prayer, public confession, charity, and baptism. But it is the Holy Spirit who enables Christians "both to will and to do of his good pleasure" (*see* Philippians 2:13).

The individual does not have to be baptized to be saved, but rather this is an outward expression of an inward reality (*see* Acts 19:5, Romans 6:3–4, 1 Corinthians 1:13–17, 1 Corinthians 12:13, Galatians 3:27, and Colossians 2:12).

The list of examples could be continued, and one must remember that some *grace-plus-work* systems are much more subtle in their approaches than others. However, the scriptural fact remains, and is presented repeatedly, that the one condition for salvation is *belief*.

There are a few verses on works, baptism, confession, etc. that may confuse an individual. However the overwhelming body of evidence points to believing as the one requirement for salvation. I should also mention that repentance does occur simultaneously with belief. Repentance literally means a change of attitude with respect to sin, self, and Christ; and this occurs as one turns away from self to Christ for salvation. Finally, belief is more than intellectual consent; belief involves a relationship with Christ.

Just as the Christian life is started in the Spirit by faith, so it is lived that way. Apostle Paul recorded,

O Foolish Galatians, who hath bewitched you, that ye
should not obey the truth, before whose eyes Jesus Christ
hath been evidently set forth, crucified among you? This
only would I learn of you, received ye the Spirit by the
works of the law, or by the hearing of faith? Are ye so foolish? having begun in the Spirit, are ye now made perfect by
the flesh?

GALATIANS 3:1–3

Stand fast therefore in the liberty wherewith Christ hath
made us free, and be not entangled again with the yoke of
bondage. Behold, I Paul say unto you, that if ye be circumcised, Christ shall profit you nothing. For I testify again to
every man that is circumcised that he is a debtor to do the
whole law. Christ is become of no effect unto you,
whosoever of you are justified by the law; ye are fallen from
grace. For we through the Spirit wait for the hope of righteousness by faith. For in Jesus Christ, neither circumcision
availeth any thing, nor uncircumcision but faith which
worketh by love. Ye did run well; who did hinder you that ye
should not obey the truth? This persuasion cometh not of
him that calleth you.

GALATIANS 5:1–8

At this point, we have to watch our tendencies carefully for
we may find ourselves fearing that a person can just accept
Christ and then live the way he prefers. We feel that he
might have the best of both lives, and that would not be
fair. Or, we may subconsciously desire to live a life in
sinful pleasure and because of a reaction formation,
whereby we do the opposite of what our subconscious desires, we impose guilt and an ungodly but rigid standard on
others. It is recorded:

For, brethren, ye have been called unto liberty; only use not
liberty for an occasion to the flesh, but by love serve one
another. For all the law is fulfilled in one word, even in this;
Thou shalt love thy neighbour as thyself. But if ye bite and
devour one another, take heed that ye be not consumed one

of another. This I say, then, Walk in the Spirit, and ye shall not fulfill the lust of the flesh.

GALATIANS 5:13–18

The life we are called to live under the principles of grace is a much higher standard than could ever be imposed by the law, because under grace and in Christ, we have the enabling power of the Holy Spirit working through us.

Reasons for Legalism

At this point, the question may arise as to why we are prone to becoming legalistic or imposing legalistic standards on others. Four apparent reasons come to my mind. The first is ignorance. If we have heard of grace-plus, or heard of grace with really some human obligation added, this may have programmed our minds toward difficulty in understanding true grace. In addition, if we ignorantly view God as human beings tend to do, we will have difficulty understanding unmerited favor. Secondly, guilt and a psychiatric concept of reaction formation alluded to previously, may be important. Reaction formations may be healthy or unhealthy. If the reaction results in a person's becoming legalistic with others because he really wants to live a loose moral life, this is unhealthy. I recall a counselee of an associate of mine. This counselee was a minister and hated hypocrisy in the church. He little realized until later in therapy, that he was very much a hypocrite himself, and was probably practicing his ministry as a result of guilt, compensation, and reaction formation. Thirdly, well-meaning individuals in their zeal may become legalistic (*see* Romans 10:2). Finally, people become legalistic for their own glory (*see* Galatians 6:12–13) and recognition.

Christ in Us

Verses that deal with the importance of our dependence upon Christ as we cooperate with His revealed Word in Scripture are:

Zechariah 4:6, ". . . Not by might, nor by power, but by my spirit, saith the Lord of hosts."

John 15:5 states, "I am the vine, ye are the branches: He that abideth in me, and I in him, the same bringeth forth much fruit; for without me ye can do nothing."

In Galatians 2:20–21 we read: "I am crucified with Christ: nevertheless, I live; yet not I, but Christ liveth in me: and the life which I now live in the flesh I live by the faith of the Son of God, who loved me and gave himself for me. I do not frustrate the grace of God: for if righteousness come by the law, then Christ is dead in vain."

It is stated in Romans 1:17; "For therein is the righteousness of God revealed from faith to faith: as it is written, The just shall live by faith."

GRACE	vs.	LAW
Salvation is a gift (Ephesians 2:8–9)		Salvation requires a payment by the individual
Demerit cannot result in salvation's being denied (Romans 5:8)		Demerit can result in denial of salvation
Personal merit cannot result in salvation's being given (Galatians 5:6)		Personal merit can result in salvation
Grace-plus nothing (Galatians 4:9)		Grace plus merit
Starts with what Christ has done (Hebrew 7:16)		Starts with what individual must do
Only believe (in Gospels over 115 times)		Believe plus. . .
Receive and then do . . .		Do to receive

GRACE	vs.	LAW
Contrasted to a. debt (Romans 4:4, 10) b. works (Romans 11:6) c. law (Galatians 5:14)		Consistent with debt, works, and law

Questions on Grace

Galatians is a book in the New Testament written by the Apostle Paul because the church at Galatia had evolved from a grace to a *grace-plus-merit* system. Paul makes several significant points concerning grace.

1. Is is possible to just trust in Christ, and then find one is not really a Christian?

No, this is not possible (*see* Galatians 2:18).

2. What is the result of combining faith with some other merit?

One sins when he combines faith with personal merit (*see* Galatians 2:18).

3. Who enables the Christian to obey God?

Christ, not the law, enables the Christian to obey God (*see* Galatians 2:20–21).

4. What happens if one feels obligated to earn salvation and does not feel Christ's righteousness is enough?

He frustrates the grace of God (*see* Galatians 2:21).

5. What does God say about those who present a *grace-plus* system for salvation?

He says they mislead others and hinder them and actually keep them from obeying the truth rather than obeying it (*see* Galatians 3:1). This persuasion is not from God (*see* Galatians 5:7).

6. Does God consider one wise or foolish who combines grace with merit?

He considers him foolish (*see* Galatians 3:3).

7. Can law (personal merit) and faith coexist?
    No, they cannot coexist (*see* Galatians 3:12, 18).

8. Since we are under grace, can anything be added to the condition for salvation?
    No, nothing can be added to the one requirement for salvation, and that requirement is faith in Christ (*see* Galatians 3:24).

9. Did the law have a useful purpose?
    Yes, the law did have a useful purpose (*see* Galatians 3:19). It still is useful in that it shows the non-Christian that he has sinned and cannot keep the law and thus needs Christ.

10. Is it possible for the *grace-plus-merit* system to give life and peace?
    No, this system cannot give life and peace (*see* Galatians 4:9).

11. How does a person feel who is in a *grace-plus-merit* system?
    He feels in bondage (*see* Galatians 4:9).

12. What does God command that Christians do in regard to a *grace-plus-merit* system?
    Cast it out (*see* Galatians 4:30).

13. If a person is to be justified by personal merit, what must he do?
    Keep the whole law, never sin (*see* Galatians 5:3).

14. Do ordinances avail anything in salvation?
    No, they avail nothing (*see* Galatians 5:6; Ephesians 2:15).

15. What does personal merit (commitments, confessions, ordinances, restitution) result in if done for salvation?
    It results in personal glory (*see* Galatians 6:14).

16. Why can one not earn salvation in just any way?

Because by definition it is a gift, and by definition, a gift is free and belongs to the recipient upon receiving it (*see* Ephesians 2:8–9).

17. Where do good works fit into God's plan?

They are a result of salvation (*see* Ephesians 2:10).

18. Is it possible for a person to "fall from grace"?

No, one cannot fall from grace (*see* Romans 11:29). According to this verse, God never takes away a gift He has given and eternal life is defined as a gift. (*see* Romans 6:23).

19. Why is it a *double-bind* message to combine grace with merit?

By definition, grace is God's unmerited favor. By definition, a gift (eternal life mentioned in Romans 6:23) is free. This means that one cannot earn grace because this would contradict the definition. Thus, when a minister asks someone to do something for the grace of God, he has just presented the individual with an impossible choice. If the individual chooses grace, he cannot do anything for it. Yet, the minister has told him that he must do something. The individual cannot win under this system. He is under a *double-bind* message.

Apostle Paul's words about aspects of this *double-bind* message are:

What then shall we say that Abraham, our forefather, discovered in this matter? If, in fact, Abraham was justified by works, he had something to boast about—but not before God. What does the Scripture say? "Abraham believed God, and it was credited to him as righteousness."

Now when a man works, his wages are not credited to him as a gift, but as an obligation. However, to the man who does not work but trusts God who justifies the wicked, his faith is credited as righteousness. David says the same thing when he speaks of the blessedness of the man to whom God credits righteousness apart from works:

"Blessed are they whose offenses have been forgiven and whose sins have been covered.

Blessed is the man whose sin the Lord will never count against him."

Is this blessedness only for the circumcised, or also for the uncircumcised? We have been saying that Abraham's faith was credited to him as righteousness. Under what circumstances was it credited? Was it after he was circumcised, or before? It was not after, but before! And he received circumcision as a sign and seal of the righteousness that he had by faith while he was still uncircumcised. So then, he is the father of all who believe but have not been circumcised, in order that righteousness might be credited to them. And he is also the father of the circumcised who not only are circumcised but who also walk in the footsteps of the faith that our father Abraham had before he was circumcised.

It was not through law that Abraham and his offspring received the promise that he would be heir of the world, but through the righteousness that comes by faith. For if those who live by law are heirs, faith has no value and the promise is worthless, because law brings wrath. And where there is no law there is no transgression.

Therefore, the promise comes by faith, so that it may be by grace and may be guaranteed to all Abraham's offspring—not only to those who are of the law but also to those who are of the faith of Abraham. He is the father of us all. As it is written: "I have made you a father of many nations." He is our father in the sight of God, in whom he believed—the God who gives life to the dead and calls things that are not as though they were.

Against all hope, Abraham in hope believed and so became the father of many nations, just as it had been said to him, "So shall your offspring be."

Without weakening in his faith, he faced the fact that his body was as good as dead—since he was about a hundred years old—and that Sarah's womb was also dead. Yet he did not waver through unbelief regarding the promise of God, but was strengthened in his faith and gave glory to God, being fully persuaded that God had power to do what he had promised. This is why "it was credited to him as righteousness." The words "it was credited to him" were written not for him alone, but also for us, to whom God will credit righteousness—for us who believe in him who raised Jesus our Lord from the dead. He was delivered over to death for our sins and was raised to life for our justification.

ROMANS 4:1-25 NIV

20. Is the individual who ascribes to law or the one who ascribes to grace the healthier mentally?

The one under grace is healthier mentally. In fact, legalism can produce serious spiritual and psychological problems. The author of Hebrews wrote that it was good for the heart to be established by grace (*see* Hebrews 13:9).

Grace—A Foundation of the Bible

When one becomes a Christian, he chooses with his will to believe in Christ. He does not necessarily need nor is he required to will a commitment beyond this, though he may. But to require a commitment beyond this is to require more than God requires.

One may pull verses out of context in the Bible and prove anything he wishes. By this, he can prove that public confession, baptism, restitution, strong commitments, and good works are all necessary to salvation. By this method he can prove that salvation can be denied because of demerit and past sins. Although men do this, when considering any work, the whole theme should be considered. The whole theme of the Bible is *grace*. The whole plot builds toward this end and is directed at this.

Grace—A Foundation of Psychiatry

In psychiatry, a foundation of therapy is that the patient feels the therapist accepts him (but not his irresponsible behavior) unconditionally. To be sure, this is the same foundation God chose for His relationship to man. To this end, Chafer, Nee, Scofield, Luther, and Spurgeon wrote about the unconditional grace of God. I personally believe this principle needs reemphasizing today. An understanding of grace is foundational to Christian psychiatry as well as to the Bible.

> ... I pray God your whole spirit and soul and body be preserved blameless unto the coming of our Lord Jesus Christ.
>
> 1 THESSALONIANS 5:23

3 A Comparison of Christian Psychiatry, Psychoanalysis, and Transactional Analysis

Psychiatry's Main Thrust

Psychiatry's major thrust has been helping an individual make appropriate changes in his soul (mind, will, and emotions) which will enable him to overcome or cope with his particular problem. For instance, psychoanalysis has dealt primarily with the subconscious (one component of the mind), as well as helping the patient understand his feelings (a function of the emotions). Transactional analysis, on the contrary, has focused on a different aspect of the mind (the logical, rational, mature, thinking aspect) and has also placed strong emphasis on the will, stating that we can determine our course in life and conquer our problems.

The Rationale Behind the Thrust

What is the rationale behind the particular thrusts of the different therapies within the field of psychotherapy or counseling? The thrust to a large extent depends upon the particular concept of the parts of man. Just what makes up a human being? The parts, and the struggle between the parts resulting in emotional conflict, are constituents of the psychoanalytic theory, the description in transactional analysis, and the description in the Bible.

57

Psychoanalytic Theory and the Parts of Man

The psychoanalytic theory holds that the important parts of man are the *superego, id,* and *ego.* These terms have become famous and are in common usage in both secular and religious settings. According to this theory, the *superego* is the conscience. The *id* represents the basic drives, such as those for food and sex. The *ego* has the responsibility of weighing between the pressures of the id and those of the superego thus acting as the logical, rational, objective, reality-oriented decision maker. Anxiety may occur as a result of striving between these internal parts of man. Consider the following diagram:

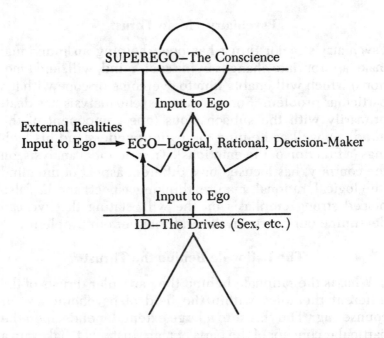

Transactional Analysis and the Parts of Man

A counselor in transactional analysis holds that man consists of a parent, a child, and an adult. The "parent" judges, the "child" emphasizes his feelings, and the "adult" acts logically and in a rational manner. In transactions with others, we are always acting and feeling like one of these entities. Consider the following diagram:

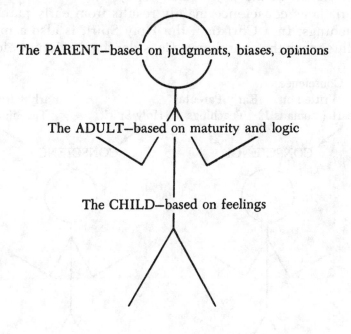

The PARENT—based on judgments, biases, opinions

The ADULT—based on maturity and logic

The CHILD—based on feelings

The Bible Versus Secular Psychiatry

The Bible, too, speaks of the importance of the parts of man, and there is a good and strikingly close correlation between the description given in the Bible and that formulated from observations and theories in psychiatry. However, there are differences. The Bible and secular theorists are alike in that they describe the struggles between the parts of man. For example, psychoanalysis describes a struggle between the drives in man (*id*) and his conscience (*superego*). The will must consider both, and also reality, and choose what to do. The Bible describes the struggle between carnal desires and the Holy Spirit in a Christian.

However, the descriptions are different in that one is a theory and pertains to man without Christ, and the other is a fact, and pertains to the Christian.

One cannot equate the Spirit in the Christian with the conscience in the psychoanalytic system because a non-Christian's conscience mainly results from early parental teachings. In a Christian, the Holy Spirit is also a major influence in the conscience. Consider the diagrams below:

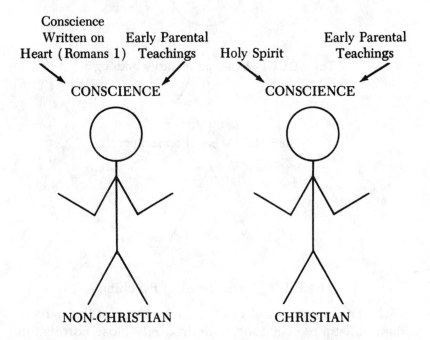

Likewise, one cannot equate the flesh with the *id* in the psychoanalytic system because the *id* by definition contains all drives. Drives can be expressed in inappropriate or evil ways, but drives in and of themselves are not evil.

Because of similar arguments, one cannot say that the parent, adult, and child of transactional analysis are parts of the soul. I would say, although most transactional analysts would heartily disagree, that the "parent," "adult," and "child" of transactional analysis are similar to the *superego, ego,* and *id* of psychoanalysis. In the diagram below similarities of the systems are noted:

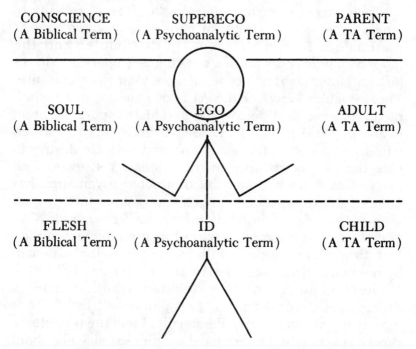

| CONSCIENCE | SUPEREGO | PARENT |
| (A Biblical Term) | (A Psychoanalytic Term) | (A TA Term) |

| SOUL | EGO | ADULT |
| (A Biblical Term) | (A Psychoanalytic Term) | (A TA Term) |

| FLESH | ID | CHILD |
| (A Biblical Term) | (A Psychoanalytic Term) | (A TA Term) |

The thrust of therapy may differ because of the importance relegated to each particular part. For example, in the past, psychoanalysis has viewed neurosis, at times, as resulting from the inhibitions of the *id*'s drive for sexual aggression. Thus, in this conceptual framework, the superego might be viewed as pathological, and therapy thus directed may be viewed as weakening the conscience. The transactional analysis, on the other hand, places much importance on the concept of the adult in each of us. Here the thrust of therapy is on the will. Likewise, the Bible speaks to the parts of man. It considers man in a whole conceptual framework. Furthermore, the thrust is on an aspect of man that psychiatry has tried in vain to avoid, namely the spiritual.

Psychiatry has tried to sidestep the spiritual aspect of

man. The secular views of the parts of man are not so er-
roneous as they are incomplete. They are ignorant of the
spiritual aspect of man. Logically, the idea of relating to
others as an adult, parent, or child at any given time is
reasonable. In fact, it seems quite simple. And the
psychoanalytic concepts of a conscience (*superego*), drives
(*id*), and logic (*ego*) do not seem more than common sense.
These secular views of the parts of man are just incomplete. As a medical doctor, the psychiatrist pays attention
to any physical problems. Likewise, he is very concerned
with the patient's mind, emotions, and will. He desires to
give the patient stability in these areas. Yet, even if all
parts of man were equal, the traditional psychiatrist has
ignored a third aspect of man. He has ignored the spiritual
aspect. *How can a third of the whole be ignored?* Can
denial be used to ignore a part of man on the assumption
that it should not be dealt with by the counselor? Can man
be fractionated and each part dealt with separately?

Theologians have long debated whether man is
dichotomous (consisting of two parts) or trichotomous
(consisting of three parts). Personally, I feel the trichotomy
theory is accurate. Others have written extensively about
these parts, but the following is a brief review.[1-8]

Man desires to be dealt with as a whole. The Bible describes the whole man as consisting of a body, soul, and
spirit. Furthermore, it describes in detail the parts of these
entities. The Bible's account of the parts of man is the most
accurate ever given. It is not based on theory or even sound
observation, but on facts. It is based on the words of the
one who made man—God Himself. An understanding of
these parts of man is basic to sound counseling. Confusion
of the functions of one part with functions of another has
resulted in much misunderstanding through the years.

Greek and Hebrew Meanings

Man consists of a body, soul, and spirit. In 1 Thessalonians 5:23 (NAS), the following is recorded: "Now may the
God of peace Himself sanctify you entirely; and may your

spirit and soul and body be preserved complete, without blame at the coming of our Lord Jesus Christ." This is a very significant verse, for it refers to three distinct and separate parts of man. The distinction is not unlike that heard in secular areas where man in totality is referred to as spirit, soul, and body. The reference is to the spiritual aspect of man, the psychological aspect of man, and finally, the physical aspect. In the above verse, each part is considered separately and thus, each has different functions; yet, they must complement to make a whole. The whole of man is again described in a very early portion of Scripture. In Genesis 2:7 NAS, the following is recorded: "Then the Lord God formed man of dust from the ground [Hebrew word for body is *basar*], and breathed into his nostrils the breath of life [Hebrew word *neshamah*, meaning the human spirit, is used here]; and man became a living being [can also be translated "soul"—Hebrew word for soul here is *nephesh*]." Thus, God combined body plus spirit to form the soul. Consider the diagram below.

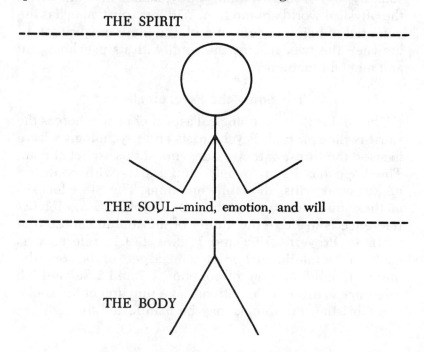

THE SPIRIT

THE SOUL—mind, emotion, and will

THE BODY

Soul or Psyche

The Greek word for soul is *psyche*. It has various meanings in the New Testament and theologians Chafer, Hodge, Vine, Nee, and Strong differ on whether it should be considered a different entity from spirit. However, I prefer to consider it as separate because of Apostle Paul's statement in 1 Thessalonians 5 quoted on the preceding page (*see* also Hebrews 4:12), and also because from a psychological view this division makes sense. It explains why Christians have emotional problems. This will be discussed later in more detail. Notwithstanding, the word *soul* is most often used as a synonym for the person—the self. In fact, translators have often translated the word *soul* as "self." Hence, Matthew 16:26 and Luke 9:25 have very similar wording but one passage records the word *soul*, and the other records the word *self.* Thus, the soul is the *self*—the person. An individual composed of spiritual capacities, plus genetic potentials, results in a unique personality, *self* or *soul*. With his body, man is in contact with the physical world around him. With his spirit, man has the potential of being in contact with the inner or spiritual. In between the two, resides the soul, with its psychological and mental functions.

The Soul—the Psychological

The soul is the psychological aspect of man, whereas the spirit is the spiritual. Psychiatrists and psychologists have focused the thrust of their endeavors at this aspect of man. The hope has been to help individuals with confused minds, weak wills, and labile emotions. The Bible focuses on these three functions of the soul. In Job 7:15 and Job 6:7 reference is made to the ability of the soul to choose (the will). In Proverbs 19:2 and Psalms 139:14 reference is made to the intellectual or knowing aspect of the soul (the mind). Finally, in Song of Solomon 1:7 and 2 Samuel 5:8 reference is made to "emotions" as a function of the soul.

A Christian's problems may be manifested through any

one of the parts of the soul. He may be very emotional, and these emotions can spring from a purely psychological base rather than a spiritual. Other Christians may become angry easily or develop bitterness quickly. In addition, a Christian's problem may be manifested through his will. He may identify with the Apostle Paul's statement, " . . . I do the very thing I do not wish to do . . ." (Romans 7:16 NAS). Lastly, the Christian's problem may manifest in his intellect—his mind. He may, like the Pharisees, know every "jot and tittle" of the law and yet be miserable. He fails to recognize that the mind alone lies in the psychological aspect of man and not the spiritual.

The soul would be a major area of attack by Satan. For an immature Christian, Satan might attack through a carnal expression of the body, such as lust-provoking sights which the eyes behold. However, for a more mature Christian he might focus the temptation a step deeper into the makeup of man and infect his soul—his mind, emotions, or will. Satan throws mental "darts" (*see* Ephesians 6) figuratively, in an attempt to establish obsessions ("strongholds") and delusions ("imaginations") in the mind of a Christian (*see* 2 Corinthians 10). Thus, Christians have mental problems and a significant percentage of patients I treat claim to be Christians.

The Christian with mental problems may, as the non-Christian, work at a disadvantage to try and handle his problems. If he is depending on his own ability, his own objectivity, or his own logic, he may very well temporarily improve. Yet, he labors at a distinct disadvantage.

The Spirit or Pneuma

This leads to a discussion of the innermost aspect of man—the *spirit*. The *spirit* is the supernatural part of man given by God at birth. It is not to be equated with the Holy Spirit of God, received by Christians at the time of conversion. The term *spirit* is used to denote several functions in the Bible.

Functions of the Spirit

There are two functions of the *spirit* about which I would like to comment. The first is that the *spirit* is the organ for communion with God. Christ stated, "But an hour is coming, and now is, when the true worshipers shall worship the Father in spirit and truth; for such people the Father seeks to be His worshipers" (John 4:23 NAS). This is why an individual can intellectually know all about Christ and yet never have experienced the joy of a personal relationship with Him.

At the time an individual comes to recognize that Christ was the Son of God—that He died on the Cross for his sins, that He rose from the grave and thus was victorious over death—and forsakes his own futile efforts to be righteous, and accepts the righteousness of God-Jesus Christ, then he becomes a Christian. When a person believes in Christ or receives Him as his Savior, then the Holy Spirit comes to indwell that person. The Holy Spirit comes to indwell that person's human *spirit* (*see* John 3:6 NAS).

Another important function of the Spirit is perception and insight. This perception comes from deep within and is independent of mental reasoning. In Mark 2:8 is recorded an instance when the scribes were reasoning, but Christ was perceiving in His Spirit. What a contrast! How can one determine if an impression is from the Spirit or just from the mind (soul)? One way is through a living knowledge of the Word of God. The following is recorded: "For the word of God is living and active and sharper than any two-edged sword, and piercing as far as the division of soul and spirit, of both joints and marrow, and able to judge the thoughts and intentions of the heart" (Hebrews 4:12 NAS).

The above paragraph is referring to the conscience as one function of the Holy Spirit. However, the Christian should remember that the Holy Spirit only makes up one factor of the conscience in a Christian and not the whole conscience. The other factors contributing to the conscience of the Christian are the early parental teachings

which were mentally healthy and the early parental teachings which were not mentally healthy (either too rigid or
not strict enough). When one understands that one of three
factors influencing the conscience of the Christian can
be unhealthy, he can understand why Christian as well as
non-Christian can have psychological problems in his conscience. The Holy Spirit's convictions are never unhealthy; neither are certain aspects of early parental teachings. However, the unhealthy aspects of early parental
teachings do produce problems. For example, parents who
are extremely strict, dominating, or legalistic produce a
child with a conscience which is always condemning him
and which he can never please. Of course, the other extreme (parents who are not strict enough) is equally harmful. Consider the diagram below:

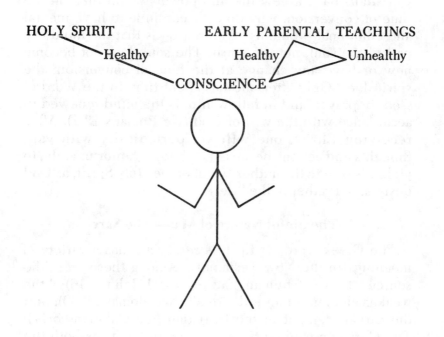

HOLY SPIRIT   EARLY PARENTAL TEACHINGS
         Healthy   Healthy   Unhealthy
                    CONSCIENCE

Why Christians Have Emotional Problems

The reasons why Christians have emotional problems are many. Genetics, environment, physical health, and stress are all factors. The importance of genetics in personality types and emotional problems is flooding the literature. With studies revealing that children of schizophrenic parents develop schizophrenia even when raised in a healthy home away from their parents, one must be impressed.[9] Likewise, literature has abounded for years with scientific evidence of the importance of environment and stress as factors contributing to emotional problems.

However, there is one factor about the Christian I wish to stress. Many problems could be avoided for the Christian if he just lived a life constantly like Christ wanted him to. He would avoid doing many things that cause guilt, anxiety, and stress. Thus, the following question arises: If Christians have a new life and power within them at the time of conversion, why do they continue to have mental and emotional problems? One reason is that the mind is a part of the soul, not the spirit. The soul does not become new or have any change at the time of conversion; the spirit does. Only after one has spent time in the Word of God, in prayer, and in fellowship, is the mind renewed in accordance with the will of God (*see* Romans 12:1). After receiving Christ, one will sin periodically with vain thoughts and actions because he chooses, unfortunately, to yield his soul to the authority not of the Holy Spirit, as God desires, but rather to the "flesh."

The Sinful Nature of Man—The Sarx

The Greek word for flesh is *sarx. Sarx* has a variety of meanings in the New Testament. Among these are: "the source of sin in human nature (*see* 1 John 2:16); "the weaker element of an individual" (*see* Romans 8:39); and the carnal element in the Christian (*see* Galatians 5:17). The Christian may be thrown into a dilemma as both the flesh and the Spirit compete for control. "For the flesh sets its desire against the Spirit, and the Spirit against the flesh; for these are in opposition to one another . . ." (Galatians 5:17 NAS).

Thus, a Christian is very complex in his makeup. Just as psychiatry has surmised, conflict between internal parts can produce anxiety. One of the best examples of the inter-relations between the parts of man in producing emotional stress was expressed by Paul:

> For I know that nothing good dwells in me, that is, in my flesh; for the wishing is present in me, but the doing of the good *is* not. For the good that I wish, I do not do; but I practice the very evil that I do not wish. But if I am doing the very thing I do not wish, I am no longer the one doing it, but the sin which dwells in me. I find then the principle that evil is present in me, the one who wishes to do good. For I joyfully concur with the law of God in the inner man, but I see a different law in the members of my body, waging war against the law of my mind, and making me a prisoner of the law of sin which is in my members. Wretched man that I am! Who will set me free from the body of this death? Thanks be to God through Jesus Christ our Lord! So then, on the one hand I myself with my mind am serving the law of God, but on the other, with my flesh the law of sin. There is therefore now no condemnation for those who are in Christ Jesus. For the law of the Spirit of life in Christ Jesus has set you free from the law of sin and of death.
>
> ROMANS 7:18–25; 8:1–2 NAS

The Law

Frustration and depression result in religious groups' trying to live by an outward law. God's salvation is not dependent upon our keeping the outward law. This is not to say that Christians disregard the law of God, but rather that people do not become Christians or remain Christians by their own power and religiosity.

The above passage from Romans records the frustration

that resulted in the Apostle Paul when he tried to keep the law in his own power. The Christian life is a supernatural life and can only be lived by the power of Christ. An individual trying to please God by his own efforts "cannot please God" (*see* Romans 8:8 NAS).

The Spirit World

Much counsel has been directed at the soul of man. However, the *spirit* is the innermost part of man and is the most important part in a Christian's search for freedom from frustration. Some people have turned to other spirits (evil spirits) for freedom from frustration. The rise of the occult is a mark of this generation. Feature articles have appeared in prominent magazines. The freedom obtained from other spirits is short-lived and results in destruction. I have had the experience of listening to young people who were at least to some degree involved in witchcraft. These young people shared a frightening story with frustrating results. Satan knows the importance of not only dealing with a person's soul (mind, will, and emotions) but also with his *spirit.*

If Christian counselors are to be effective, they must not only help their clients find psychological freedom, but they must realize that only Jesus can give and maintain real freedom and peace of mind. This peace of mind begins with a rebirth in one's spirit by accepting Christ and continues as Christ's influence spreads outward from the spirit to change the soul (mind, emotion, will).

Part II

Recognizing Emotional Problems

For God hath not given us the spirit
of fear; but of power, and of love, and
a sound mind.

2 TIMOTHY 1:7

4 Mental Health and Mental Illness

Definitions

The terms "mental health" and "mental illness" are used much today, but are really quite vague and general terms. These terms mean different things to different people. In fact, to a degree, they mean different things to different psychiatrists. Thomas Detre and Henry Jarecki have given the best in-depth criteria I have read concerning "mental health." The reader is referred to their book.[1] However, in brief, I have offered below some broad definitions and some areas of agreement among psychiatrists for diagnosing emotional problems.

An individual is considered mentally healthy if he is in contact with reality and is sufficiently free of anxiety so that he is not significantly incapacitated functionally, socially, or biologically for any extended period of time. He is not so uncomfortable that he develops a prolonged sleep problem, becomes socially withdrawn, and has trouble at his job. This individual can still function emotionally without being unduly uncomfortable for a prolonged period of time.

In contrast, an individual with a clear-cut mental health problem may have lost contact with reality; or be so filled

with anxiety that he suffers significantly biologically, socially, and functionally. Symptoms that all people have
(anxiety, fear, depression, worry, guilt, body aches and
pains, etc.) increase in magnitude and occur more often in
these individuals. Their biologic functions (sleep, appetite, sex) are impaired. Their social interaction suffers.
Other people may note that something seems wrong. They
may be functioning poorly in their jobs. If a person has
significant trouble in three basic areas (biologic, social,
functional) beyond a transient period, he has a mental
problem. Below are the chief complaints of individuals
who did suffer significantly in these three areas:

"I feel unwanted."

"Not able to sleep . . . head-crawling feeling."

"I stay depressed most of the time. I am very high-
strung."

"Lonely and pain."

"Recurring nightmares and listlessness . . . I don't have
any real ambition."

"An inability to cope with stress."

"Fear of doing something . . . unreal feelings . . .
wicked dreams and thinking."

"Depression, apathy, loss of contact with reality."

"Life in general is dull or else threatening."

"Nervous."

"I feel symptoms of weakness and tiredness."

"Nervous tension and confusion."

"Depression and inner conflicts."

"Psychological addiction to intravenous amphetamines."

"Depression and drinking."

"I have what is called a dual personality."

"Dizziness, fainting spells."

"Headaches . . . unable to handle my father . . . he puts
pressure on me about my marriage."

"Drinking since mother's death."

"Drinking."

Defense Mechanisms—
Healthy and Unhealthy Ways to Handle Anxiety

The above are typical chief complaints indicating anxiety. These anxieties were manifested in various problem types such as patients with depression, psychosis, and hysterical trends. In fact, the way anxiety is handled often determines the type of mental problem that develops. The particular way the individual handles the anxiety is determined by defense mechanisms.[2,3]

Defense mechanisms often operate on a subconscious level. Thus, one may not be immediately aware of the reason he does something. And, if he is not careful, he may justify inappropriate behavior and even sin.

Some defense mechanisms are good and healthy, but others are not. For example, *projection* can be an unhealthy defense mechanism by which one attributes to someone else his own thoughts and feelings. A Christian who reacts drastically to specific faults in others may actually be projecting his own faults. In 1 Samuel 19 is recorded the story of Saul wanting to kill David. Undoubtedly Saul felt very threatened by David and felt David wanted to do away with him. The truth was that Saul wanted to do away with David.

CASE 1:   Mrs. A. stated that men *always* flirted with her. I wondered if she was not projecting her own desire to flirt and imagined the flirting was coming from the men.

In the above case, as in all cases presented, specific details are not used. In many, insignificant details have been changed or deleted.

A second defense mechanism is *reaction formation.* Through a reaction formation, an individual does exactly the opposite of what he would like to do. For example, a reformed alcoholic may become the spokesman in the community against alcohol. Also, a minister may evidence this if he repeatedly speaks against pornography. In addition, a sociopath might become very religious. Clearly, the Pharisees were outwardly very pious, but inwardly they were near reprobates. Another example is found in Proverbs 13:24 where the case of a parent who never spanks or disciplines his child is recorded. Hatred is said to be the reason for the lack of discipline. In other words, a parent who would literally like to beat his child to death may go to the opposite extreme and not spank at all.

CASE 2:   Suzie was an eight-year-old girl who was repeatedly setting fire to the house. The mother refused to discipline the girl. Psychiatric evaluation and history revealed she had resentment toward the girl and was undergoing a reaction formation.

Rationalization is a defense mechanism that many use to avoid responsibility. Not only is there a danger of rationalizing irresponsibility but also sin. Abraham lied about his wife Sarah, David committed adultery with Bathsheba, and Solomon built temples for idols. Even these godly men rationalized to permit their behavior; yet, their rationalizations cost them much. Hopefully, we will learn from these lessons of history.

A fourth defense mechanism is *introjection*. Introjection is often used by depressed individuals to assume responsibility for events outside their realistic control. This explains why depressed individuals so often feel guilty when they are truly guiltless. Introjection in adults is usually unhealthy; however, one case when healthy introjection did occur in an adult was Christ's introjecting the responsibility for our sins upon himself (*see* Matthew 27:46).

CASE 3:   Joe felt guilty when he found his boss having an affair. Joe had had nothing to do with the whole situation, and yet he felt personally responsible and guilty.

A fifth defense mechanism that certainly should be mentioned is *repression*. Repression is basic to all other defense mechanisms. Repression is the involuntary exclusion of unwanted thoughts from consciousness. Thus, an unwanted thought, such as the true reason for an inappropriate behavior, is first repressed and then a second defense mechanism is used such as rationalization to justify the inappropriate behavior.

A sixth defense mechanism is *suppression*. Suppression is the conscious analogue of repression. It is the voluntary exclusion of unwanted thoughts from consciousness. To pay attention to one idea one must exclude many others that would pop into the mind. Students use suppression during Christmas holidays to enjoy the season and not worry about school. Of course, this is often healthy.

A seventh defense mechanism is *compensation*. By compensation one excels in one area because he feels inferior in another.

CASE 4: Bill felt inadequate in sports. He compensated by making excellent grades in school.

An eighth defense mechanism is *idealization and identification*. This is the overestimation of desirable traits in another. Many students do this with their professors. Christians are particularly prone to find someone other than Christ to idealize. This is not to say that we should not identify with or imitate other Christians. Apostle Paul told the Philippians to imitate him as he imitated Christ. (*See* Philippians 3:17.)

Isolation is the splitting off of an emotion from an event or thought. By this, many individuals with obsessive-compulsive personalities avoid being in touch with their emotions. They seem to endure disturbing events with little emotions. Of course, the emotions are there; they are just not in touch with them.

Displacement defends the individual by shifting the emotional component of one event to another event or person. This explains why, when a man has a difficult day at work, he explodes at his wife the same night. Hysterics often displace anxiety onto their bodies by developing various physical problems.

Often, how and when they are applied determines whether they are detrimental. For example, learning to sublimate our instinctive drives into actions for Christ is a step toward maturity. Also, the defense mechanism of *identification* may be healthy and is scriptural. The Apostle Paul asked others to imitate him as he imitated Christ.

Knowing the above and other basic defense mechanisms will help in considering the mental problems soon to be discussed. One can predict with a good deal of accuracy the defense mechanisms that will be used by an individual with a particular mental problem. For example, the hysteric will usually use denial and displacement. The obsessive-compulsive will usually use isolation, reaction formation, undoing, and magical thinking. The schizophrenic uses fantasy and regression. The paranoid uses projection. The depressed person uses introjection.

Diagnosing Mental Problems

There are those who feel that psychological problems do not exist. I believe this is due to a lack of understanding; for if the mind, emotion, and will do exist, and if individuals ever have problems in one of these areas, then psychological problems exist by definition. By biblical definition, the soul is the mind, emotion, and will; and by biblical documentation even godly men had significant problems in one of these three areas resulting in depression (*see* Psalms 32) and even psychosis (*see* Daniel 5:21).

There are also those who suggest that psychiatric diagnoses should no longer be used but rather, that degrees of irresponsibility should be determined. This would make communication among mental health workers such as psychiatrists, pastors, and social workers extremely difficult. Two terms such as *paranoid schizophrenia* or *involutional melancholia* can tell me literally volumes, whereas a colleague telling me a patient was moderately irresponsible would tell me little.

I agree that mental health workers should be extremely careful when using psychiatric diagnoses, but to go to the other extreme is equally harmful and unreasonable.

Mental problems can be broken down into ten major categories.[4] These categories are: *mental retardation, organic brain syndrome, psychosis* (a loss of contact with reality), *neurosis, personality disorders, psychophysiologic disorders, special symptoms, behavior disorders of childhood and adolescence, transient situational disturbances*, and conditions without manifest psychiatric disorder (and nonspecific conditions).

Each of the above categories is dealt with briefly below. The more interesting problems are discussed in depth in later chapters.

Mental Retardation

A person is considered mentally retarded if his I.Q. is 85 or below. The degree of retardation is designated as follows:

Type	I.Q.
Borderline mental retardation	68–85
Mild mental retardation	52–67
Moderate mental retardation	36–51
Severe mental retardation	20–35
Profound mental retardation	under 20

The causes of mental retardation are numerous: infection, intoxication, trauma, physical agent, disorder of metabolism, disorder of nutrition, brain disease, chromosomal abnormality, prematurity, psychosocial deprivation, etc.

CASE 5:   Q. was a 14-year-old boy brought in to see me by his father. The boy had a long history of both physical and emotional problems. Thus, the father desired a psychiatric evaluation. The father stated the boy first developed problems in the second grade after being hit by a car. This resulted in a blow to his head. Soon afterwards, the boy developed problems in school. Then he developed severe peptic ulcer disease and had had several surgeries for this. The evaluation revealed the boy had border-line mental retardation. He also had some schizophrenic symptoms. With supportive psychotherapy, antipsychotic medi-cation, and appropriate school placement, he adjusted well. It was interesting to note in this case that the one uncle also suf-fered from latent schizophrenia. Another interesting fact was the conflict that had existed between the patient and his parents. He had been smothered by one and deserted by the other.

Organic Brain Syndrome

The five cardinal symptoms of this syndrome are: Intellect—impaired, Memory—impaired, Affect—flat, Judgment—impaired, and Orientation—impaired as to person, place, time.

The individual with *organic brain syndrome* may be either psychotic or nonpsychotic, and the condition may be either acute or chronic. The causes of this condition are many: alcohol, drugs, syphilis, encephalitis, presenile de-mentia, senile dementia, brain trauma, cerebral ar-teriosclerosis, cerebrovascular disturbance, epilepsy, metabolic disorder, and poison. The degree of organicity varies from mild to severe.

Organicity can often be picked up by asking the patient to repeat a few digits in reverse order after the counselor. It can also be found by asking the patient to remember four objects for a few minutes. The patient with organic brain syndrome will have trouble doing either of these.

CASE 6:   Mrs. C. was brought to see me by her daughter. The daughter was concerned about her mother because the mother's memory had become progressively poor over a ten year period.

The mother would also become very irritable at times which was inconsistent with her previous disposition.

Upon psychiatric examination, this eighty-six-year-old patient was not oriented to the specific month. She could not remember any of four objects after a few minutes. She could recall only a few digits forward and none in reverse. Both her judgment and intellect were impaired. She had no history of schizophrenic symptoms.

The diagnosis was *organic brain syndrome, chronic, nonpsychotic.*

CASE 7:   Mr. B. came to see me to obtain a psychiatric evaluation for the purpose of obtaining his private chauffeur's license. He had had a history of heavy drug use during his adolescence and thus, this evaluation was required. Often, heavy drug use results in organic brain syndrome.

During the evaluation, the patient was well-oriented. His memory was excellent. He did well when asked to subtract serial sevens from one-hundred. He did have a few errors on the Bender test which is used to detect organicity.

The patient was fortunate. He had escaped significant organicity. Several interesting facts came to light in this case. He was raised by his mother alone since his father was killed in the war. During his early adolescence, he was heavily involved in drugs and the occult, factors which exacerbated his rebellion. However, during late adolescence, the patient accepted Christ as his Savior. His life began to change. He stopped using drugs, got a job, finished college, and eventually married a stable and dedicated Christian girl.

Psychosis

Psychosis is simply a loss of contact with reality. Scripture records the story of a man, King Nebuchadnezzar, who had this problem.

> But when his heart was lifted up, and his mind hardened in pride, he was deposed from his kingly throne, and they took his glory from him: And he was driven from the sons of men; and his heart was made like the beasts, and his dwelling was

with the wild asses: they fed him with grass like oxen, and
his body was wet with the dew of heaven; till he knew that
the most high God ruled in the kingdom of men, and that he
appointeth over it whomsoever he will.

DANIEL 5:20-21

I was the admitting physician at a mental hospital for a
year. The above description of Nebuchadnezzar reminded
me of the men I admitted. They would come into the hospital for admission during the middle of a cold night. They
were unkempt, and at times, no doubt were literally "wet
with dew from heaven"! Also, they would eat anything.
Again, I'm sure some would literally eat "grass like oxen."
(*See* Daniel 5:20–21.)

Psychosis is probably best described by discussing the
three divisions of this problem: *schizophrenia, major affective disorders*, and *paranoid states*.

SCHIZOPHRENIA which includes counselees with "strange
experiences," accounts for most of the psychoses. It has
been characterized through the years by four A's. They are:
having a flat affect, having loose associations, being ambivalent, and being autistic. These individuals have a
thought disorder which is often reflected in loose associations in their conversation. Below is a note written by a
schizophrenic:

I'm a grandfather with six sons and a daughter who *loves* watching your work. I wish to extend the use of our small acreage and
horses cows dogs and cats, and pure Arkansas air and creek A
wife and crew of boys who may be useful

Jack

I love children and always have.

In addition to their loose associations and flat facial expressions, their ambivalence goes beyond normality to extremes. Secondary symptoms such as hallucinations (seeing or hearing things not present) or delusions (beliefs
contrary to solid facts) are often present. Schizophrenia is
broken down into eleven subcategories.

Simple Type: This is characterized by social withdrawal, *regression*, and *autism*. Some hoboes would fit this category.

CASE 8:   Miss. I. came for an appointment as an outpatient. She seemed shy, withdrawn, socially regressed, and autistic. She had never been able to hold a job for any length of time. She still lived with her parents. She had very few, if any, close friends. She had never dated. Subsequent psychiatric evaluation revealed that this patient had simple schizophrenia. With supportive psychotherapy the patient did begin to improve.

Hebephrenic Type: This is characterized by silliness and extreme regression.

CASE 9:   A thirteen-year-old girl was brought by her parents for an evaluation. The parents said that the girl had always been a quiet girl, but very stable. She had suddenly started acting in a strange and irrational manner.

Upon psychiatric evaluation, she would not respond appropriately to questions. Her facial expression was extremely inappropriate. She would stand in front of a mirror and giggle as she gazed at herself.

The patient was found to have schizophrenia. Hers was childhood type because she was very young. However, she had hebephrenic symptoms.

Catatonic Type: This may be characterized by extreme withdrawal to the degree that the patient will not even move. By contrast, some catatonics may become very excited with much uncontrolled activity.

CASE 10:   A young lady was admitted to a psychiatric ward because of her sudden break with reality. She was extremely withdrawn. In fact, she would maintain her extremities in whatever position they were placed.

On the other hand, another schizophrenic patient had to be watched carefully to keep him from harming himself by suddenly falling backwards or making some other excitatory movement.

The first case illustrates the *withdrawn* catatonic schizophrenic, while the second case illustrates the *excited* catatonic schizophrenic.

Paranoid Type: This is characterized by the patient's being excessively suspicious and often hostile. The patient has the usual symptoms of schizophrenia, but he is also delusional and paranoid. He may really want to harm others but he projects his feelings onto others and feels they want to harm him.

CASE 11:   A middle-aged male came for an appointment because he was referred by a Christian Counseling Center. He presented with the fear that his wife was trying to kill him. He had no proof of this, but his suspicions were strong. For example, his wife had asked for a vacation from her job. She had told him she wanted to take a vacation with him and get the marriage back together. When the wife commented that her boss had granted the vacation and even said, "Take however long it takes," the patient was sure this meant she was going to kill him. He was also very worried about his wife's wedding vow, "Till death do us part."

Subsequent psychiatric interviews revealed the extensive delusional system this patient had built. He also had a history of auditory hallucinations. He felt he had heard Christ speaking to him and calling his name. This patient had paranoid schizophrenia.

Acute Schizophrenic Episode: This is characterized by the acute onset of a thoughts disorder and loss of contact with reality. The patient has no previous history of schizophrenia and often recovers in a short time.

Latent Type: This is characterized by symptoms of schizophrenia and yet, a clear-cut psychotic break has never occurred. These are borderline cases.

CASE 12: A father brought his son in for a psychiatric evaluation. The boy was found to be schizophrenic.

Some very interesting observations were made during the interview with the father and son. Not only was the boy schizophrenic, but the father seemed schizoid also. The father had never had a psychotic break or any other diagnosed mental problems; however, his conversation revealed somewhat loose associations. His affect was inappropriate. He would tell of a tragic event and smile. He seemed autistic. Some ambivalent feelings about the boy were present. In short, he had the four A's of schizophrenia.

I felt the father was a latent schizophrenic.

Residual Type: This diagnosis is reserved for patients who have had psychotic breaks but are no longer overtly schizophrenic.

CASE 13: A 28-year-old black female presented at my office with the desire to start psychotherapy. She gave a history of having had a psychotic break at one time. During that time, she heard voices, had a rich fantasy life, showed poor judgment, and did strange things like walk around the block in her pajamas. At the time of the interview, she was not overtly psychotic. However, her associations did seem a little loose, and her affect was a little inappropriate. Psychiatric evaluation revealed she had schizophrenia, residual type.

This patient's history was very interesting and deserves comment for it shows the danger of an unstable early environment. Her mother and father divorced when she was very young. She moved often as she was growing up, first living with both her mother and father, then only with her mother, then with her grandparents and then with her stepfather. Her uncle tried to rape her when she was twelve years old. Her mother drank a lot. The history goes on and on in this fashion.

Of course, Christ did change the direction of her life. She became a Christian around twelve years of age and grew both spiritually and emotionally through her involvement in a local church.

Childhood Type: This diagnosis is applicable when schizophrenia occurs in childhood. These children may be autistic, regressed, withdrawn, or have inappropriate behavior.

CASE 14:   James was a ten-year-old white male who had been admitted to the psychiatric unit at the request of state authorities. James had threatened to kill his mother and grandmother with a shotgun. James had always related very poorly with his peers and was socially very regressed. While he was socially very regressed, he did run the home and would become enraged when his desires were thwarted. Psychiatric evaluation revealed that he had extremely poor judgment, was very autistic, and was not in contact with reality. He was schizophrenic, childhood type.

Chronic Undifferentiated Type: This patient has various schizophrenic symptoms (paranoia, depression, withdrawal, etc.). Because he has various symptoms, he does not fit in any one particular category, so he is defined as an "undifferentiated type."

CASE 15:   Mr. E. had been in a psychiatric ward for twenty-five years. He was one of the few patients who had never been able to return home from the hospital. His loose associations, his inappropriate affect, and his bizarre behavior had gone on so long that they had been ingrained into his personality. He was one of the sad cases who had suffered from chronic, undifferentiated schizophrenia.

Schizo-Affective Type: This type is characterized by the schizophrenic's being either very euphoric or very depressed or alternating between the two.

Other Types: This category is reserved for schizophrenics who do not fit one of the other categories.

CASE 16:   Carol was referred to me by her minister. The pastor said the girl had been very active in church and had been a very intelligent young lady. Suddenly, during a church service, she rose from her seat and began to wander through the auditorium. The pastor talked with the girl and noted her entire personality had changed. She was withdrawn, had a flat expression on her face, and acted in a bizarre manner. During the psychiatric interview the girl revealed that she felt that God had called her to enter the state psychiatric hospital so she could share the gospel with the other patients.

The patient was found to be a schizophrenic, but it did not fit under any of the first ten categories listed above. With supportive psychotherapy, antipsychotic medication, and gentle care from her local church, she began to improve.

MAJOR AFFECTIVE DISORDERS may be characterized by a loss of contact with reality, but the primary presenting problem seems to relate more to a mood disorder. This will be evident by the descriptions of the subcategories below:

Involutional Melancholia: This is characterized by severe depression (possibly to delusional proportions) beginning in middle age.

CASE 17: Mrs. G., a forty-five-year-old white female, presented to the psychiatric unit with extreme depression and suicidal thoughts. Psychiatric interviews revealed she had no prior history of depressive episodes or any other mental problems. Psychiatric evaluation revealed this lady to have *involutional melancholia.*

Manic-Depressive Psychosis—the euphoric counselee: This is characterized by the patient's being either manic (extremely euphoric, hyperactive, having pressure of speech, etc.), depressed, or cycling between the two.

CASE 18: Sue was a twenty-two-year-old housewife who had been admitted to the psychiatric unit because she was extremely euphoric and was also showing very poor judgment. She had a history of a *manic-depressive* illness. She had had several manic episodes. During one of these episodes, she thought she was the

Virgin Mary. During another, she walked down the street nude.

During the psychiatric evaluation, I noted how "high" the patient was. And although she was "high," she could become very hostile in an instant. Her speech was very rapid as was her motor activity. She showed very poor judgment during her first several days in the hospital.

The patient was started on Lithium and within a few weeks she appeared perfectly normal. This further supported my feeling that this patient did indeed have the *manic* phase of *manic-depressive* psychosis.

PARANOID STATES are forms of psychoses. Obviously these patients have lost contact with reality through their paranoid delusions. The descriptions below will clarify the subdivisions.

Paranoid: This is characterized by an elaborate delusional system. Other than this one elaborate system, the patient has no major mood or thought disorder.

CASE 19: Mr. H. felt the Mafia was after him. I was in my residency training and was listening intently to a professor as he interviewed this man. Although the man had no evidence for his fear and although the professor explained in a very logical manner to Mr. H. why the Mafia could not be after him, Mr. H. held firmly to his delusion. Other than this one delusional system, Mr. H. related well and his associations were appropriate.

Involutional Paranoid State: This is characterized by the paranoid delusions' beginning in middle life.

Other Paranoid States: This category is reserved for those psychotic paranoid states not fitting under the other two categories.

Neurosis

Neurosis is a less severe mental problem than psychosis. Whereas psychosis is characterized by a loss of contact with reality, *neurosis* is characterized by functional incapacity to some degree. *Neurosis* is caused by anxiety, and how that anxiety is handled often determines the subclassification of the neurosis. The following diagram illustrates neurotic manifestations:

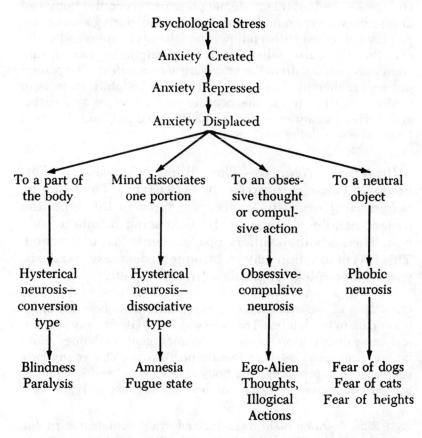

Anxiety Neurosis—The Anxious Counselee: This neurosis is characterized by *free-floating* anxiety. The patient feels fearful and panicky. One patient's anxiety led to episodes of fear and hyperventilation.

CASE 20: Betty was a twenty-one-year-old college student who came for a psychiatric evaluation due to episodes during which she would become very anxious, hyperventilate, and think she was going to pass out. In addition, Betty had a great deal of *free-floating* anxiety.

Psychiatric evaluation revealed Betty had an *anxiety neurosis*. Several precipitating causes were discussed. First, Betty was in college and feeling the academic pressure. Secondly, Betty had always been a very moral, Christian girl and, during a weak moment, went to bed with a fellow. She felt very anxious and guilty over this. Of course, other than these precipitating causes, subconscious conflicts from the past were also manifest. The patient did well in therapy. She also found help in Scripture memory in dealing with her fears. She became very active in a Christian group. Her anxiety episodes gradually faded out, and the last I heard, she was doing well.

Hysterical Neurosis—The Blind Counselee: This neurosis is characterized by one of two types. The first type is *hysterical neurosis—conversion type*. In this type, the patient handles his anxiety by displacing it onto a body part. The body then suffers a psychogenic loss of function. This loss of function may be blindness, deafness, paralysis, paresis, hemiplegia, aphasia, convulsions, etc.

CASE 21:   L. was admitted to a psychiatric ward because of intense pain in her left leg. The pain was not related to any anatomical nerve distribution and no significant organic pathology could be found on physical examination or by x-ray. The young lady gave a life history of various body aches, pains, and symptoms. She was diagnosed as *hysterical neurosis-conversion* type.

CASE 22:   A young male was admitted to a psychiatric ward due to episodes during which his personality would completely change. He would develop a personality much different from his usual personality type. The patient was usually a moral and conscientious young man, but during these states, he would curse, smoke, and act in a manner contrary to his usual personality. At this point, some readers may be thinking "demon possession." However, this man responded and improved with a matter-of-fact psychotherapeutic approach. His multiple personalities ceased.

Obsessive-Compulsive Neurosis—The Counselee with Ego-Alien Thoughts: This neurosis is characterized by the patient's handling his anxiety by diverting it to obsessive thoughts or compulsive actions. The obsessive thoughts are ego-alien. For example, the godly John Bunyan, who wrote *Grace Abounding to the Chief of Sinners*, had the distressing recurring thought of "sell Christ."[5] He had persistent unwanted thoughts and urges to irrational actions. This is *obsessive-compulsive neurosis.*

CASE 23:   Tom was a thirty-year-old white male who came for an appointment because he was depressed. Several precipitating causes (financial problems, business problems, religious confusion) were discussed. However, the really interesting dynamics to this case came out when the patient discussed his past.

He described his parents as very strict disciplinarians. When he was young, his parents would spank him at times, and at other times, wash out his mouth with soap. While still in grade school, he developed the compulsion to wash his hands. He would wash his hands repeatedly and would avoid touching things so his hands would not get dirty. Because of these symptoms, the parents consulted a child psychologist who suggested that the parents not be so hard on him. They took his advice and the symptoms largely disappeared. However, even today, he said he would wash things often, wrap food several times, and is very perfectionistic.

The dynamics of the case could be explained as follows:

Stressful early-life situation (domineering parents)
↓
Anxiety produced
↓
Anxiety repressed into subconscious (which can be called Anxiety 1)
↓
Stressful current-day situation arises (financial and business pressures)
↓
Anxiety produced (which can be called Anxiety 2)

Anxiety 1 also aroused

↓

Anxiety displaced to compulsive action

↓

Anxiety 1 also aroused by Anxiety 2

There are thus actually three levels of anxiety with which to deal in counseling: Anxiety 1, Anxiety 2, and Anxiety 3.

With psychotherapy the patient began to let up on himself, relax more, fret less, and be less serious. As he began to improve, so did his confusion over Christianity. He began to stop blaming God for his depression. He began to realize God was not trying to punish him. He stopped reading so many religious books for answers and turned to the Word for spiritual nourishment.

CASE 24:   Dora was a twenty-year-old lady who came to see me with the chief complaint of depression. However, the psychiatric interview revealed there was much more involved than just depression. Dora felt she must repeatedly ask God to forgive her for every moment-to-moment bad thought or action. She had become immobilized. She even doubted the sincerity of her request for forgiveness and would then have to ask God to forgive her for that. Her daily quiet times had turned from worship to hours of inward introspection. On one occasion, Dora felt the compulsion to curse over the phone and did so. This was the last thing she consciously wanted to do, and she felt very grieved. Her symptoms had even gone to the point that she thought she heard voices on one occasion. She was profoundly depressed and was near overt psychosis. Her diagnosis was *obsessive-compulsive neurosis.*

Recognizing the patient had three problems (physical, psychological, and spiritual), I started therapy. First, through medication, I began to attack the biochemical abnormalities present. As the patient's physiology returned to normal, she started to make progress. I also instructed her to limit her devotional time to five minutes per day for the time being. She was reminded that this was for worship, not introspection. She was encouraged in therapy to be less rigid, less serious, and less introspective. The last time I saw her, she had adjusted and was doing very well. She was still a very dedicated Christian, but now she had balance.

CASE 25: Caroline was a very dedicated Christian girl. She came for an appointment because she wanted guidance about a spiritual issue.

She felt compelled to make apologies to everyone. She would apologize for the least little matter. This was beginning to get her into trouble in certain areas. For example, she was a nursing student, and when she kept apologizing to a teacher for not reading every word of an assignment, he became angry with her. Rigidity and perfectionism characterized every aspect of Caroline's life. Through therapy, she was able to begin to see this and even laugh at it a little. She seemed a little shocked when I told her I felt that her feeling so guilty over any mistake or fault was more a matter of pride than humility. Someone would have to be almost omnipotent to cause the reverberations she felt she caused with the slightest error. Through therapy, she was able to begin to see that the real issue was not the compulsion to confess, but that this was only a symptom of some deeper subconscious anxiety. In other words, in an attempt to control some subconscious anxiety, she had displaced it from its original source to the compulsion to confess. She began to relax more, have more fun, become more involved with other young people at church, and to steadily improve.

CASE 26: Beth, a twenty-five-year-old white female, came to see me due to guilt feelings. She felt guilty about everything. She felt guilty over a minor scratch she might cause to a car. She felt guilty for leaving a dripping faucet on. She felt guilty over throwing away a tissue paper for fear it might have contained a contact lens. She felt guilty for a college teacher's giving her a grade that was too high.

She also worried about her hands being dirty after touching a door knob. She worried about making some mistake at her job that would cost the company money. All of these traits are *obsessive-compulsive*.

As with hysterical neurosis and schizophrenia, people through the years have often been quick to say that an individual with an *obsessive-compulsive* problem is demon possessed. Thus, a few words on demon possession may be useful at this point. There is today an upsurge of interest in the topic of demon possession. Prominent magazines have had feature articles dealing with the occult. The film *The Exorcist* is among the top films in amount of money grossed. Young people, not finding solutions to their problems, are turning to the supernatural.

On the one hand, I believe the occult is a mark of our age. On the other hand, much of what is suspected to be demon possession could be one of three psychiatric problems—hysterical dissociative reaction, obsessive-compulsive neurosis, or schizophrenia. Because of the current interest in demon possession, much confusion will result, not unsimilar to the widespread confusion that existed in the fifteenth century when the *Malleus Maleficarum* was written to help in the diagnosis of witches and demon possession. Unstable individuals, impressionistic, hysterical personalities, and borderline schizophrenics could believe they were demon possessed after watching a film similar to what I am told the *The Exorcist* is. Psychiatrically-based dual personalities and obsessive-compulsive neurotics will be mistaken for being demon-possessed individuals.

Safety for the Christian is not found in being overly interested in demon possession but in having a renewed interest in Christ our Lord. Because of the confusion of our day, only a living knowledge of God's Word will give stability. The pursuit of God, God's Word, prayer, and fellowship with godly people—these are the solutions.

Phobic Neurosis: The Counselee with Irrational Fears: This neurosis is characterized by the anxiety's being diverted to an animal or object. Thus, an individual may have an extreme fear of dogs, cats, or heights. He may recognize the absurdity of his fear but cannot help it. His fears are irrational.

The dynamics of phobic neurosis could be explained as follows:

Stressful early-life situations

↓

Anxiety produced

↓

Anxiety repressed into subconscious (which can be called Anxiety 1)

↓

Stressful current-day situation arises, producing Anxiety 2

↓

Anxiety displaced to phobia (fear of elevators, heights, and so on)

↓

Anxiety produced, secondary to worrying over the phobia (which can be called Anxiety 3)—individual attempts to control Anxiety 1 and Anxiety 2 with the phobia which produces Anxiety 3

Actually, then, there are now three levels of anxiety with which to deal in counseling: Anxiety 1, Anxiety 2, and Anxiety 3. I believe all *three* levels of anxiety should be dealt with. Some schools (behavior modification) deal mainly with Anxiety 3 and help the person to overcome his irrational fear through desensitization. Other schools (some religious counselors) deal mainly with Anxiety 2 and help the person to deal with the present-day situational problem. And yet other schools (psychoanalytic) deal mainly with Anxiety 1. I feel that all three anxiety levels must be tackled.

Perhaps this can be more clearly seen in the obsessive-compulsive neurotic who fears committing the unpardonable sin. Again, all three levels of anxiety must be dealt with in counseling. Certainly, the subject's intense Anxiety 3 of committing the unpardonable sin must be dealt with by the use of Scriptures. The counselee also needs help with Anxiety 2 and his present-day situational problem. Finally, Anxiety 1 and the early childhood fears must be handled.

Depressive Neurosis: The Depressed Counselee: This neurosis is characterized by the following feelings: blueness, sadness, helplessness, hopelessness, and worthlessness. The patient is to some degree functionally incapacitated by his symptoms. For example, many patients with this problem find they awaken early in the morning hours and are unable to go back to sleep. The patient looks sad, feels sad, and has trouble functioning socially and biologically. Often the patient is reacting to the loss of a love object (relative, self-esteem, etc.).

CASE 27:   Mr. M., a twenty-five-year-old white male, came for a psychiatric evaluation due to depression. He described his mood as one of hopelessness and helplessness. He stated he was so depressed he had trouble sleeping. Mr. M. said he had not had any plans for suicide but that he had felt desperate. He gave an interesting history. He said his father had always been very melancholic and timid. He said he was a lot like his father.

During therapy, I initially listened and tried to help the patient gain insight. However, much of the therapy was focused on helping him change his depressive mood by changing his behavior. After a few sessions, the patient began to improve significantly. He listed the following things he felt helped him:

- He gained insight into things he was doing to hurt himself; into the fact that he had learned depression from his father and could, therefore, "unlearn" it; and into some detrimental defense mechanisms he was using (denial of angry feelings, *introjection* for responsibility of events beyond his realistic control, and projection of his feelings onto others to avoid getting close to them).
- He made a decision to change.
- He began looking for positive things to do rather than negatives to avoid. He chose to take the initiative in making friends and to be more assertive when appropriate.
- He began taking antidepressive medication which restored his body physiology to normal.
- He began memorizing verses such as Psalms 43:5 and Genesis 4:6–7.

- He began doing things he had decided were important, things such as writing letters and cleaning his closet.
- He began realizing what his personality traits were, and therefore began to understand that he needed more "strokes" from others.
- He decided that through Christ he definitely was OK.

CASE 28: Mrs. N. came for a psychiatric evaluation because she was very depressed. She felt blue, sad, and hopeless. She had a sad facial expression. In short, she had the four classic symptoms of depression: sad affect, painful thinking, psychomotor retardation, and anxiety.

Mrs. N. had just gone through an acutely stressful situation, and the depression resulted. With therapy (including ventilation and insight both psychological and biblical), she improved. Her plans to work on the depression had included:

- Get up by 7 A.M. regardless of how I feel.
- Fix my husband's breakfast three times a week.
- Avoid watching soap operas.
- Visit a friend two times a week.
- Memorize Jeremiah 15:18 for depression.
- Have a daily devotional time.

CASE 29: Mrs. S. presented with the chief complaint of a drinking problem. I soon detected that in this case her drinking was the result of depression. Her husband had recently died.

Thus, in this case, the depression was exogenous (caused by external factors) rather than endogenous. She had suffered the loss of a love object which is the usual cause of exogenous depression.

With antidepressive medication and psychotherapy she improved. Her plans to help herself had included:

- Continuing to work daily
- Getting involved in a local church
- Visiting daughter more
- Going out with friends
- Reading a verse of Psalms daily
- Praying daily
- Being more assertive

CASE 30:   Mrs. J. was an elderly lady who had recently moved to a new city. Thus, she had lost her friends, and her previous interests, and had become depressed.

I listened to Mrs. J., helped her gain insight, and aided her in making practical plans to change her behavior and thus, her feelings. She became involved in the women's missionary society. She developed new interests and stopped staying home watching soap operas. She spent more time with her grandchildren. Needless to say, the depression lifted.

Hypochondriacal Neurosis—The Counselee with Pains: This neurosis is characterized by the patient's diverting or displacing his anxiety onto various body parts and functions. The patient fears his body will develop some disease.

Neurasthenic Neurosis—The Weak Counselee: This neurosis is characterized by a person with low energy levels and a chronic state of fatigue.

Depersonalization Neurosis—The Counselee with Feelings of Unreality: This neurosis is characterized by feelings of unreality and depersonalization.

Other Neuroses: This category is reserved for any neurosis that does not fit one of the above listed categories.

Personality Traits and Disorders

All individuals have certain personality traits. Most people have a spread of different personality traits with perhaps a predominance of one. This is healthy. On the contrary, one particular personality trait may lead into a personality disorder. This is not healthy. A personality disorder is characterized by: being lifelong, manifesting a particular life-style (mentally unhealthy and maladaptive), and by the excessive use of certain predictable defense mechanisms in order to handle anxiety.

Galen (130–200 A.D.) felt there were four personality

types in man.[6] Of late, these four personality types have been made popular by Tim LaHaye in his book *The Spirit-Controlled Temperament.* These are sanguine, choleric, melancholic, and phlegmatic. The sanguine was the outgoing, extroverted, likeable type person. He tended to be emotionally unstable under pressure. The choleric was the cold, formal leader. The melancholic tended to be depressed at times and was a very sensitive person. The phlegmatic was easygoing and cool.

Biblical characters illustrate many of the traits without having a disorder. For example, Apostle Peter demonstrated hysterical traits at times with his emotional immaturity. On the other hand, Apostle Paul demonstrated obsessive-compulsive (perfectionistic) traits with such statements as those recorded in Philippians 3:4–6. Furthermore, Moses illustrated explosive traits at times. Once he exploded and killed an Egyptian. Another time, he exploded and it cost him the Promised Land. He also demonstrated cyclothymic (depressive) traits at times. Also, King Saul demonstrated paranoid traits which he later carried to overt psychosis. Also, Abraham demonstrated passive-aggressive traits when he was told that his wife was his sister. In fact, he did this twice because he feared that if the pagans knew she was his wife, they would kill him. He was passive rather than dealing with the problem directly. Finally, Judas demonstrated sociopathic (criminal) traits. He undoubtedly had a winning personality as do many sociopaths. He carried the purse for the group and made living arrangements for the entire group. He would have had to get along well with people. But he was manipulative, lacked much of a conscience, and showed no guilt until the very end.

When one carries a trait to an extreme, it becomes a disorder. Below are descriptions of personality disorders.

Hysterical Personality—The Emotional Counselee. The diagnostic manual for psychiatry uses ten terms to describe an hysterical personality. They are excitability, emotional instability, overreactivity, self-dramatization, attention seeking, seductive, immature, self-centered, vain, and dependent.

Thus, an individual with an hysterical personality develops a life-style early in life characterized by self-centeredness, manipulation, and seduction. This life-style has persisted with the patient throughout life.

A typical example is not hard to find (even in the Christian community) of a young, attractive female who dresses seductively and is immature.

An individual with hysterical traits is usually attractive, likeable, and has a winning personality. He or she, just as the rest of the body of Christ, needs to have his or her personality molded by the Spirit of Christ. The following is an example of a female who had recently become a Christian and was very dedicated. She wanted to be a good wife, but her hysterical personality and sexual frigidity were causing her family problems.

CASE 31:   Mrs. P. presented with the chief complaint of anxiety. She presented her story rather dramatically, and was attention seeking, and seductive in her actions. She gave a history of emotional instability and overreactivity. She seemed immature and self-centered.

The psychiatric history revealed several important facts. First, she had been married once, but had gone out on her husband numerous times. Also, she had attempted suicide several times.

CASE 32:   Mrs. R. presented a similar history to that of Mrs. P. except she also gave a history of having been raped by her uncle. Mrs. R. had been married twice.

CASE 33:   Mrs. T. also presented with an hysterical personality as did the two above. Her reason for admission was especially interesting. She had taken two aspirins to kill herself. Obviously, this was a manipulation tactic.

CASE 34:   Mrs. U. was an hysteric who made her suicide attempt just as her husband was passing by on the street.

CASE 35: Mrs. V. had often gone to bed with men, but she had never had an orgasm. In fact, she did not like sexual intercourse.

CASE 36: Mrs. W. had done poorly in therapy until I changed my attitude to more of a matter-of-fact approach. I refused to be manipulated and refused to give her attention for inappropriate behavior. I encouraged her to think more and go less on the whims of her emotions. With this approach, she began to improve.

All of the above cases illustrate important factors and dynamics in the hysterical personality. These are discussed in more detail in a later chapter.

Obsessive-Compulsive Personality—The Perfectionistic Counselee. These individuals are characterized as being perfectionistic, being intellectual, and having oppositional thinking.

First, these individuals are perfectionistic in many ways. They do their jobs and do them well. In fact, they work too hard, are too dutiful, are too conscientious, and are unable to relax. They are neat, clean, orderly, and meticulous. They are concerned with details in their work. They never feel they have done enough.

Secondly, these individuals are intellectual. They are concerned with facts, not feelings. In fact, they have trouble expressing how they really feel but are great at intellectualization. They seem cold, formal, and rigid. They could argue at length on how many angels could sit on the head of a needle. They are logical, rational, and cautious but are lacking in flexibility.

Not only are these individuals intellectual, they tend to be oppositional in their thinking, which can make therapy difficult. If one said, "Yes," on a subject, they would tend to think, "No." And the reverse would also be true. This complicates their problems with authority. On the one hand, they have a need to conform and usually seem overly meek and compliant, but on the other hand, they resent this. Since they tend to always disagree, the problem with authority is further complicated. Finally, because they split hairs and cling to tiny distinctions, their problem with authority is accentuated.

Most successful people have some of the above traits. However, if extended from a trait into a personality disorder, the trait can control an individual.

Apostle Paul is an example of an individual who had many obsessive-compulsive traits and was used very effectively by God. Apostle Paul wrote of himself:

> Circumcised the eighth day, of the stock of Israel, of the tribe of Benjamin, an Hebrew of the Hebrews; as touching the law, a Pharisee; Concerning zeal, persecuting the church; touching the righteousness which is in the law, blameless.
> PHILIPPIANS 3:5, 6

Of course, God taught the Apostle Paul to depend on Him, not on his own natural abilities, but God transformed and used that personality for His glory.

CASE 37:   Mr. S. was very successful in the business world. He was successful because of his perfectionism. However, his being perfectionistic had begun to get him into trouble. He could no longer relax. He was having trouble controlling his anger.

Through therapy he began to relax more and stopped carrying his perfectionism to the extent of being overly dutiful, overly conscientious, and overly concerned. He controlled his anger better. He stopped worrying so much about what others thought.

Paranoid Personality—The Suspicious Counselee. These individuals are characterized by being overly suspicious. They do not trust others. Actually, they may have evil motives which they cannot admit to themselves, so they project them onto other people. Thus, if they feel hatred toward someone, they feel that that person does not like them. We dislike in others what is often present in ourselves.

These traits do make one sensitive and discerning and thus, can be helpful if not carried too far.

King Saul is one biblical example of an individual who certainly had many paranoid traits. He became very hostile and overly suspicious at times. However, his problem went beyond a personality disorder. His problem makes interesting reading and is recorded in 1 Samuel.

Cyclothymic Personality—The Moody Counselee. These individuals are characterized by being either depressed, elated, or alternating between the two. When these individuals are feeling high, they have a bubbly personality, are outgoing and likeable. They have a tremendous amount of energy and can be very successful. They are doing a dozen things at once. When these individuals are feeling low, they are sad, blue, and feel hopeless and helpless.

Schizoid Personality—The Loner. These individuals are characterized by being shy and socially regressed and withdrawn. They would often rather be alone and may seem to be caught up in their own thoughts, daydreams, and fantasies.

Explosive Personality—The Explosive Counselee. These individuals are emotionally explosive when provoked. They have outbursts of temper and may become violent. The individuals with these trends, I have seen, are usually likeable and have good personalities until put under emotional pressure.

CASE 38: Mr. A. was usually a nice guy. In fact, at one time, he had been a minister. He had a very likeable personality.

Mr. and Mrs. A. were interviewed together, and Mrs. A. revealed that, at times, her husband would just explode as he became intensely angry. Mr. A. confirmed this. He was found to have an explosive personality.

Antisocial Personality—The Criminal. These individuals are characterized by a lack of conscience, or, at least, an impairment in this area. Thus, they do not feel guilt for wrongdoings. Furthermore, even though they may go through repeated conflicts with the law, they do not seem to learn from experience. These individuals are likeable and have winning personalities. In addition, they are manipulative so they are good at conning people. These individuals feel little responsibility toward anyone but themselves. They feel they are "OK" and everyone else is not "OK." They are more likely to resist the gospel than any other one group.

CASE 39:   I recall one young man who was on his way to prison if he should do anything else in conflict with the law. The patient seemed to feel no guilt and did not learn from his experience. He continued to be irresponsible and do things in direct conflict with the law. He was eventually sent to prison.

CASE 40:   Mr. B. came to see me at the request of his sister. I immediately noted his winning personality. He told of a lifelong history of drug abuse, frequent job changes, divorce, etc.
   After evaluating the patient, I told him he did not have a psychosis nor a neurosis. Rather, he had a problem in his personality and needed to begin to make some changes in his behavior patterns. At that point, he was no longer interested in therapy.

CASE 41:   Mr. C. came requesting medication for anxiety. He had a history of drug abuse. When I refused to give him the drugs, his interest in therapy suddenly left.

Both of the above cases were of men with antisocial personalities. They were not really interested in therapy and certainly not in changing.
   This personality type is similar to that described in Romans 1 of the "reprobate mind." The following terms are used to describe the reprobate mind in Romans 1 (*see* Romans 1:29, 31): "unrighteous, wicked, covetous, malicious, full of envy, murder, deceit, and without understanding."

The following chart compares the description of the Bible with that of psychiatry.

Psychiatry	Bible
1. Repeated conflict with society	1. Murder, deceit, disobedient to parents
2. Incapable of loyalty to others	2. Full of envy, spiteful, covenant-breakers, backbiters
3. Selfish	3. Covetous, full of envy, proud, boasters
4. Callous	4. Filled with unrighteousness
5. Not able to learn from experience	5. Without understanding

Passive-Aggressive Personality—The Passive Counselee. These individuals are characterized by often being very passive in their responses to others. They have learned to accomplish their desired ends by passive means. They may be stubborn, pout, put things off, be late, and use various other *passive-aggressive* techniques.

CASE 42: I had been in therapy with Jack, a teenage boy, for several sessions. I had tried everything I knew to get the boy to open up, but he would not. He was determined to be *passive-aggressive* as teenagers often are. I decided I would be passive also and not speak until he did. After ten minutes or so my supervisor (during my residency) interrupted. We were making *him* nervous. This is often the case in therapy with passive-aggressive individuals. They can be hard to work with at times.

Inadequate Personality—The Inadequate Counselee. These individuals are characterized by just being generally inadequate in many facets of their lives. Often they are socially inadequate and have problems dealing effectively with others in interpersonal relationships. They are inadequate in handling stress. They may even seem both mentally and physically adequate although they are not. Psychiatry uses the following terms to describe this personality: "ineffectual responses to demands, unadaptability, ineptness, poor judgment, and lack of physical and emotional stamina."

Of course, we all have some areas of inadequacy, and in Christianity, Christ can use one's inadequacies to His glory (2 Corinthians 12).

Asthenic Personality—The Fatigued Counselee. These individuals are characterized by being generally weak and fatigued. They have low energy levels. They may have various body aches and pains.

Occurrence of These Disorders in Marriage

The above information concerning personality traits and disorders is perhaps most useful in marriage counseling. Numerous combinations could be formed. However, several of the combinations seem to occur more often and have been described in detail.[7] Of course, most marriages will not be as sick as the ones listed below. However, many of the traits may be present in a less severe form.

One of the most common types of marriages in America is the obsessive-compulsive man and the hysterical woman. The obsessive-compulsive man is dutiful, conscientious, and concerned and has a strict conscience. He is attracted to a female who is somewhat the opposite of him in many ways—a girl who is emotional, excitable, dramatic, theatrical, and seductive. He finds this dramatic, emotional, seductive nature pleasant at first. She arouses pleasurable emotions in him.

Likewise, she is attracted to him since he has many opposite traits than she. She likes his nonemotional, stable, logical, father-figure image.

Each finds in the other what he lacks. He lacks emotions.

She arouses this in him. She lacks logic and stability. She likes the apparent stability she finds in him. Thus, while they can really complement (since he can't feel and she can't think), they may begin to become irritated with each other. He may grow tired of her dramatics, and she may grow tired of his cold logic. If both are relatively immature, the stage is set for a lifelong battle of conflicting personality traits.

A second type of marriage is the passive-aggressive husband married to the passive-aggressive wife. Both are passive and immature. Both want to receive more than they give. Both are overly dependent. Neither is able to understand the needs of the other because they are so self-centered.

I recently had one such couple in marriage counseling. Both claimed the other was immature, self-centered, childish, and just wanted his own way. They seemed surprised when their psychological test showed they were extremely similar in personality type. Indeed, both were immature and self-centered. They had been unable to recognize it in each other and had been blinded to their own personal problems.

A third type of marriage that is often seen in America and is based on a neurotic attraction is the passive husband and the dominant wife. Each feels a neurotic need of the other. He has a need for someone to lead, to be in charge, and to dominate. She has a need to lead, to control, and to dominate. Conflicts arise because he is inwardly hostile at being dominated, and she is frustrated by not having her own dependency needs met. This too is a parent-child type interaction, but here she is the parent and he is the child.

A fourth type of marriage is that of the paranoid husband and the depressive wife. This is the sadomasochistic type relationship. He is jealous, hostile, angry, and has a need to hurt others. She is prone to depression, has a low self-image, and readily accepts blame. In short, she has a need to be hurt. His main defense mechanism is *projection* by which he attributes his own shortcomings to her. Her main defense mechanism is *introjection* by which she assumes blame for things she didn't do. Often, the female in this relationship had critical, demanding parents. She subconsciously sought out the same type of parental figure in the man she married. Accepting blame became a way of life.

A fifth type of marriage is the paranoid wife and the depressive husband. It is just the opposite of number four above. In this relationship the wife is angry, hostile, and paranoid. The man has a low self-image and readily accepts blame. The same sadomasochistic neurotic needs exist as above. She has the need to hurt others, and he has a need to be hurt. In a warped sort of way, accepting blame gives the depressive husband a little self-worth. He feels like he is nothing, but he can't be a nothing if he is responsible for so much.

A sixth type of relationship is the asthenic wife and the obsessive-compulsive husband. She is sick (both mentally and physically) and has a need for someone to totally take care of her. He feels inadequate in the world and has a need to take care of someone who is weaker than he is. Conflicts arise because she begins to resent being totally dependent on someone else, and he begins to resent the drain he feels from her continuing sickness.

A seventh type of marital relationship is that of the obsessive-compulsive husband and the obsessive-compulsive wife. Both may be overly perfectionistic, demanding, and critical. Thus, they can hardly live with themselves and certainly have difficulty with each other. Of course, if they are relatively healthy with their obsessive-compulsiveness, they can have a very orderly marriage.

The technique of counseling will be dealt with in a later chapter. Let it suffice here to say that the marriage counselor has various roles. He is a listener. He is an observer of communication patterns. He is one who confronts and points out games and detrimental defense mechanisms. He helps the couple gain insight into their personality types. He helps them to formulate specific plans of action to deal with their problems.

Psychophysiologic Disorders

This disorder includes more mental problems than any other category. This disorder is a cousin to a conversion reaction in that the anxiety is handled by displacing it onto a body function. The difference is that the autonomic nervous system, not the voluntary nervous system, is involved. Thus, a system under control of the autonomic nervous system is involved so that the patient would experience a gastrointestinal disorder (ulcers, gastritis, constipation), a respiratory disorder (asthma, hyperventilation or hiccoughs), a skin disorder (pruritus, dermatitis), or a musculoskeletal disorder (backaches, headaches). There is actual organ pathology but the cause is emotional. The problem could be diagrammed as follows:

Hereditary Factors

↓

Early Environmental Factors (Social, Religious, Physical)

↓

Detrimental Defense Mechanism Develops at Early Age by Which Anxiety Is Handled by Displacing It Onto a Body Function

↓

Acutely Stressful Situation

↓

Anxiety

↓

Hypothalamus of Brain Affected

↓

Autonomic Nervous System Affected

↓

Specific Organ Influenced

↓

Organ Pathology

↓

Psychophysiologic Disorder

CASE 43:   Mr. C. had intense abdominal pain. He had had extensive medical evaluations, and no physical cause could be found.

Psychiatric evaluation revealed Mr. C. had had an argument with a supervisor just prior to the onset of the abdominal pain. The argument had resulted in a loss of job status for Mr. C. This resulted in intense angry feelings and anxiety. Mr. C. had displaced the anxiety to his abdomen.

Special Symptoms

This category is reserved for symptoms and problems not classified elsewhere. It includes such problems as speech disturbance, learning disturbance, tics, sleep disorders, bedwetting, and feeding disturbances such as *anorexia nervosa*, in which there is voluntary weight reduction to the point of death, at times.

Behavior Disorders of Childhood and Adolescence

This category includes the mental problems that arise during and before adolescence. The problems range from transient situational reactions to psychosis.

Transient Situational Disturbances

This diagnosis is applied to someone who is basically emotionally healthy. However, because of a transient, acutely stressful situation, the patient has developed emotional problems and symptoms.

Conditions Without Manifest Psychiatric Disorder and Nonspecific Conditions

This category is reserved for those individuals who do not have a manifest psychiatric disorder yet, but need counseling. Examples would include marital maladjustment and social maladjustment.

In summary, one must be incapacitated in several areas (biologically, socially, functionally) before I would diagnose him as mentally ill.

Factors Causing Psychological Problems

There are several factors which are important in the development of a mental illness.[8] These factors and the various forms of the development of mental illness are diagrammed below:

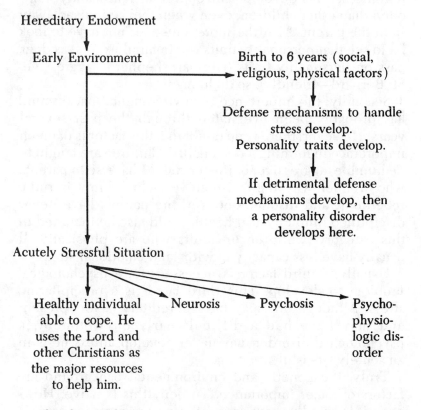

Hereditary Endowment

Early Environment

Birth to 6 years (social, religious, physical factors)

Defense mechanisms to handle stress develop.
Personality traits develop.

If detrimental defense mechanisms develop, then a personality disorder develops here.

Acutely Stressful Situation

Healthy individual able to cope. He uses the Lord and other Christians as the major resources to help him.   Neurosis   Psychosis   Psycho-physio-logic dis-order

A book could be written on the importance of each one of the diagrammed factors in the development of mental illness. Mental illness is not so simple and often is not caused by one factor alone. A spiritual problem may be the cause of the emotional problem, but other factors often come into play or are responsible.

For example, the genetic background is important when

examining a mental problem. I have seen one mental problem in particular, *manic-depressive psychosis,* where an unusually high proportion of the relatives had also had the problem. And, as stated elsewhere in other chapters, scientific studies have documented that children of schizophrenic parents develop schizophrenia significantly more often than other children, even when they are raised away from the parents.[9] Furthermore, one does not have to look far to see that personality traits run in families. Just as dogs pass on personality traits (German shepherd—aggressive, St. Bernard—friendly), so do humans.

Secondly, the importance of environmental background has probably been overstated through the past several years. However, there is no doubt that this factor is of much importance in forming a personality. Children are taught to be humble, aggressive, polite, or rude. I have seen parents who wonder why their sixteen-year-old Johnny is rude, rebellious, and disobedient. Yet, the parents have never disciplined him. Physical health could also be included in this category. Children or adults who are physically ill usually have less capacity to withstand emotional stress.

Usually, a third factor is necessary for a psychological problem to develop. This third factor is a precipitating stress. Although one may have hereditary factors present and may have had a difficult early environment, a psychological disorder may never develop unless he is in an acutely stressful situation.

Truly, the genetic and environmental background are factors of major importance. To deny this is naive. However, it is equally naive to use these as excuses for present conduct. Many problems are brought about through irresponsible behavior. What Apostle Paul said many years ago is still true: ". . . whatsoever a man soweth, that shall he also reap" (Galatians 6:7). Many times emotional problems are brought about through irresponsible behavior, sins, or just not knowing, or failing to rely on the resources that a Christian has at his disposal.

The counselor needs certain criteria
by which to reach conclusions concerning the counselee and his personality trends.

THE AUTHOR

5 The Evaluative Workup

The counselor needs certain criteria by which to reach
conclusions concerning the counselee and his personality
trends. These criteria are given below under the titles indicated.[1] I believe there is a potential danger in the following information. This information is not given so that we
can analyze everyone we meet or ourselves. This can be
"soulish" and dangerous; and further, we may exercise our
own "soulish" powers rather than relying upon the Spirit
of God.

*May we submit our knowledge to the guidance of God
and pray that what we discover can be used to help the
counselee to grow in Christ.*

Circumstances of Referral and Presenting Problem

This is simply a statement of who the counselee is, and a
brief statement usually in the counselee's own words of
what he understands his problem to be. An example would
be: "This twenty-four-year-old white male from Jonesboro,
Arkansas, was referred to me by his minister, Reverend
John Ward. The patient's chief complaint was 'depression.'"

113

History of Present Problem

Under this heading the counselor goes into more detail about the presenting problem. The counselor will need to know when the problem first started, if there were previous episodes, the duration of the episodes, what helped to relieve them, who was previously sought as a counselor, what medication was used, and what event, if any, precipitated the problem most recently. In addition, current symptoms that are present and the severity of these symptoms are very important. Also, the counselor will need to know the current events contributing to the problem, and how the counselee has attempted to deal with these events and his problems.

Past History

A past history often reveals significant data which aids in understanding and helping the counselee. While the focus is not on the past, the counselor would be omitting significant data to ignore the past entirely.

First, data concerning the counselee's birth and early development should be considered. Data obtained here can reveal insight into the cause of a learning disability, mental retardation, and other mental problems. The nature and duration of the mother's pregnancy, the birth weight, complications at birth, the age at walking and talking, and the living situation at the time of birth are all significant.

Secondly, data relating to the family can be very helpful. The counselor will need to know the parents' age, health, current residency, and most importantly, a description of each of their personalities. The relationship the counselee had with each parent is also very important. Not only is data relating to the parents helpful, but data relating to siblings is helpful also. The number of siblings, the relationship with the siblings, and the order of birth are all important. From this kind of data, the counselor can learn much about the counselee's personality, about how he relates and even about how he may view God inasmuch as we tend to view God as we view our genetic parents.

Thirdly, the events that occurred during school should be considered. What kind of grades did the counselee make? How much study did this require? Did he have many surface friendships or a few close ones? What were his main interests? When did the counselee start dating? Did he graduate from high school? And if so, when? Did he attend college? What were the major events that happened during the college years? From such data, the counselor can be alerted to such factors as underachievement or overachievement tendencies. This may explain why he has tension at his job. Also, from such data, the counselor can determine how the counselee relates to people. He can note whether the counselee's educational level and functional level correlate.

Fourthly, there are several other areas about which the counselor will need data. Was the counselee in the military service and, if so, what type of discharge did he receive? What is the counselee's occupation? Does he have a history of changing jobs frequently? How many times has he been married? What does the patient list as the causes for any previous divorces? Is the counselee's spouse in good health? How do they relate? How are they compatible? How are they different? Does the counselee have children? How old are they? Are they in good health? Does the counselee have a history of drug abuse? Does he have a history of conflicts with the law? From such data, the counselor can learn about the emotional stability of the counselee in general. He can learn if he has sociopathic tendencies. He can learn about various stress factors heretofore not discussed.

Finally, a history of the counselee's relationship to Christ is very important. Has the counselee accepted Christ as his Savior? Does he know how one becomes a Christian? How has he grown spiritually through the years? What does he do for spiritual growth now? Would his strongest area be Christian fellowship, Bible study, prayer, or witnessing for Christ? Which of these four areas does he need to grow in most?

Evaluative Examination

The first parameter in an evaluative examination is *general appearance*. Does the counselee appear to be his stated age? What is his demeanor? Is he tense, suspicious, grave, slouchy, dignified, manneristic, or gracious? What is the condition of his clothes? What is his general behavior: Is he restless? Is there any strange or unusual behavior present? The answers to these questions determine much.

If a counselee appears older than his stated age, he may have spent many years obsessively worrying. When he appears many years younger, with few, if any, wrinkles, he may be a schizophrenic, for he may have escaped anxiety through the years by escaping reality. If the counselee appears suspicious, he may have paranoid trends. Noting that a counselee is meticulously dressed gives a clue that he may have obsessive-compulsive tendencies, and thus guilt may be one of his problems. If the counselee is rather unkempt, he may be depressed. When depressed, men stop shaving, and women stop fixing their hair and putting on makeup. If the counselee is obese, he may be depressed and is compensating by overeating. When the counselee is seductive in dress and action, an hysterical trend exists and also, perhaps immaturity. When the counselee has grease on several areas of his tie, he may have an organic brain syndrome inasmuch as most people would rid themselves of such a tie. If the patient shows unusual behavior, he may be psychotic. For example, he may keep looking around as though he is hearing or seeing something. If he is restless, overt anxiety is present for some reason. Observing that a counselee will not look up, holds his head down, alerts the counselor to think of depression. Whether the counselee's greeting is vigorous, seductive, or warm tells much. If the counselee has a history of much antisocial behavior, but the therapist is drawn to like him, he may be a sociopath. When the counselee steps into the office and does not close the door, or is late for the appointment, he has passive-aggressive tendencies.

If the counselee is an adolescent, the counselor should be cautious about making an official psychiatric diagnosis since the normal adolescent *is* abnormal! To be sure, adolescence is a time of many adjustment reactions which present in many ways.

If the counselee is a young child, the counselor will want to know the relationship with the mother. If the child is in the age range of four to twelve, the counselor will especially focus on the parent of the same sex, since the child is at a stage of introjecting into his personality the attitudes of his parents, especially the one of like sex. When the counselee is in his fifties or sixties and has always been very productive and conscientious, but has suddenly become depressed, the counselor thinks of an involutional melancholic process seen often at this age. In the old, the counselor is especially apt to look for organic causes.

In counselees with physical problems, the counselor should be aware of possible depression. If the counselee appears shy, aloof, and introverted, the counselor may think of schizoid trends. If he demonstrates low frustration tolerance and an outburst of verbal abuse, the counselor has clues to explosive trends that are present and poorly controlled. When the counselee presents himself as a result of marked anxiety at work, and the counselor notes ineffectual responses to questions, the counselor will consider that the counselee is producing beyond his capabilities and thus frustration is resulting.

Most of the above parameters are picked up by evaluation of general appearance and can be helpful in determining the personality trends, and thus, potential problems of the counselee.

The second parameter in a mental examination is *intellectual proficiency*. Is the counselee oriented to time, place, and person? How many digits can he recall immediately after they are presented to him? Six to seven forward is average. How is his memory of both recent and remote events? How is his knowledge of general information compared to his educational background? Can the counselee subtract serial sevens from one hundred; can he divide one hundred by seven? Has he had any periods of amnesia?

These questions indicate whether an individual has an organic brain syndrome. This would be important in evaluating the aged. They would indicate whether he could concentrate or was preoccupied with other thoughts as in depression. They would indicate roughly his I.Q. and thus give valuable information concerning overachievers.

The third parameter is *communication*. What is the rate of conversation? Is the conversation logical or does the counselee ramble? Is the conversation relevant? Can the counselor follow the train of conversation of the counselee, or are there loose associations present? Is the conversation spontaneous or resistant? Does the thought content make sense? Can he interpret proverbs, demonstrating he is capable of abstract thinking? Does the counselee have an obsession or preoccupation? Has he ever heard voices?

If the counselor cannot follow the conversation of a counselee, but rather the associations are loose; and the counselee cannot interpret a simple proverb as "Don't cross a bridge until you get to it"; and he reports hearing voices, the counselor may strongly suspect schizophrenia. If the counselee cannot rid himself of thoughts that are foreign to his usual thinking, he may be obsessive-compulsive. If the counselee has had periods of amnesia, he may have a type of hysterical symptom. If the counselee speaks spontaneously, he tends to be extroverted. On the other hand, he may only answer questions, a tendency indicative of being introverted.

The fourth parameter that an evaluative examination includes is *mood*. How does the counselee describe his mood? Does he say he is happy, sad, or indifferent? Does the counselee cry often? What is his facial expression? Is his expression consistent with the way he describes his feelings? Has the counselee made any suicidal gestures? Has he ever felt like life was just not worth living? How is the counselee sleeping and eating? If he is married, what is the sexual relationship between him and his spouse?

A counselee may describe his mood accurately or he may not; therefore, other parameters are important. For example, a depressed person may have trouble going to sleep, or he may awaken in the early morning hours. His appetite is usually poor. If the counselee has made several unsuccessful suicidal gestures, he may be hysterical rather than depressed. Thus, the counseling would be totally different. An individual may have a flat affect. If so, depression or even schizophrenia is a consideration.

I hope the above criteria are helpful, but they must not be overread. The evaluative examination depends on many factors and a life history of how a person functions socially and biologically.

The Impression

This is simply a statement of what the counselor feels the real problem is. It is usually very short such as *depression*, or *adjustment reaction*, or any one of numerous descriptions.

Dynamic Formulation

In the dynamic formulation, however, the counselor attempts to integrate all he has learned about the patient (hereditary factors, environmental factors, basic personality type, defense mechanisms, religious history, and precipitating events) into a cohesive explanation of how the counselee has evolved up to the present. An example would be the following hypothetical case of John Doe, a *manic-depressive*.

"Hereditary factors do seem to be important in this case. Three of John's relatives have also suffered from *manic-depressive* problems. However, early environmental factors cannot be ignored, as reference to past history has proved. In short, hereditary factors combined with early environmental factors to produce detrimental defense mechanisms and ways of coping. When John was subjected to increased stress last year with the death of his father, he decompensated into a *manic-depressive* episode. Since that time, John was led to Christ by a friend. He has become involved in a local church and now is beginning to cope well."

What follows is an outline of a typical Evaluative Workup:

The Evaluative Workup

   I. Presenting Picture

  II. History of Present Problem

 III. Past History

 IV. Evaluative Examination

  V. Impression

 VI. Tentative Dynamic Formulation

VII. Initial Counseling Plan

Signature

"Though I say, 'I will forget my complaint I will leave off my *sad* countenance, and be cheerful,' I am afraid of
all my pains."

JOB 9:27–28 NAS

6 Physical Condition and Emotional Problems

The Whole-Person Concept

A counselor is responsible for considering more than the surface mental or emotional problem that an individual presents. Man consists of a body, soul, and spirit, and each must be considered. Physical disease and problems may affect the mental capacities of a person and produce emotional problems. Likewise, spiritual problems can affect the mental functioning of an individual and produce emotional problems.

Related Problems

First, a person's physical condition should be considered in any apparent emotional disorder, whether it pertains to mild depression or psychosis. For example, rather early in my residency in psychiatry, I was assigned to manage a lady who was overtly psychotic. I greeted the lady and then listened as she rambled on in religious jargon. Her speech was rapid, and she seemed "high." I had had previous cases of *manic-depressive psychosis*, and from my impression, she fit this condition. In short, an individual with the manic phase of *manic-depressive psychosis* would be apt to have extreme elation, flight of ideas, pressure of

121

speech, impaired judgment, and delusions. The delusions may center around religious or sexual preoccupations. My patient fit this description. Later, in the course of discussion, a relative revealed that the patient had been treating herself for nervousness with an over-the-counter medication. This particular medication was prone to produce these symptoms when taken in excess. After several days the patient had eliminated the medication from her system, and her symptoms cleared.

Hyperactivity in children is another example of an apparent emotional problem that may really be physical. There is a neurological impairment that results in hyperactivity. If not placed on medication, however, secondary emotional problems may develop. When placed on appropriate medication, the hyperactivity decreases, and the child is able to sit still and concentrate as other children do. The hyperactivity is not the result of an emotional problem of the child nor of inadequate child care by the parents. I should mention that all cases diagnosed as "hyperactive" are not always hyperactive because of physical causes; therefore, emotional causes may need to be sought. Definite neurological signs and other factors must be considered in making a correct diagnosis.

CASE 44:   Johnny was a typical example of a hyperactive child. He could not sit still in school, had a short attention span, and poor concentration. John was considered a "bad" boy and a trouble maker.
I saw John and found him to have moderate signs in a neurological examination. The rest of the evaluation also confirmed the diagnosis of a neurologically based hyperactivity problem. John was started on medication and the teachers quickly noted the change. Johnny began to pay attention in class. His concentration improved. He was not so disruptive.

Educators are being alerted to this problem, and today these children are often recognized and thus referred for help. Such was not the case until recently.

Schizophrenia is another example of an emotional problem which may have a physical base. Children may also be schizophrenic or autistic since infancy. This would indicate again a primary biochemical or physical problem. Children with a schizophrenic family heritage are more apt to develop schizophrenia than the average child. Even when raised apart from his genetic family, a child of schizophrenic parents still has a significantly higher chance of developing schizophrenia than the rest of the population. Again, this indicates that physical factors are important.

Hypoglycemia is another condition which may cause nervousness, or even a marked change in personality. This may result in diabetes mellitus from an overdose of insulin or insulin-releasing agent. It also may result from an organic cause or may be functional. If the cause is simply functional, which is often the case, the problem can be helped by relieving stressful situations, eating more often, and eating more protein than carbohydrates.

Although hypoglycemia does exist, I should point out that it has been overemphasized among Christians. I feel that hypoglycemia as a cause of emotional problems has been overemphasized.

Hypothyroidism and *hyperthyroidism* are glandular physical problems which may manifest emotional disorders causing nervousness.[1] Hence, the hyperthyroid patient may present as a thin, excitable, nervous person. Mental symptoms vary from exhilaration to severe depression. In contrast, the hypothyroid patient may present as overweight and slow, but also nervous. In either case, with proper treatment both improve greatly.

Among the many physical diseases which may also carry an emotional component is *mononucleosis*. It is well known that individuals suffering from this may develop depression.

CASE 45:   Harry was such a case. He had been a good student for two years in medical school. He then developed mononucleosis. After he recovered, he suffered from depression and for a while had a difficult time with his grades.

Physical Stress is a physical problem that results in psychological problems. It is not as rare as the above, but a condition common to most at some time. Physical exhaustion may beget or accentuate emotional problems. Christ Himself knew the importance of rest after a hard day of work (*see* Mark 4:38).

In the discussion of physical problems causing emotional symptoms, one more condition deserves comment because of its prevalence during old age. This is the problem of *organic brain syndrome*, which ranges from very mild to severe in advanced years. Because of such physical factors as increased arteriosclerosis in the brain, or *Alzheimer's disease*, these individuals are more emotionally labile, less flexible in their opinions, and may lose some of their usual restraints. Also, undesirable personality traits may become more prominent. Individuals having this syndrome manifest *accentuation* of basic personality traits and *release* of previous inhibitions. Of course, these individuals need more patience from others.

In summary, almost any physical problem can accentuate emotional problems. The ability to cope with daily stresses is greatly decreased in physical illness. Thus, the hyperactive child will be much less likely to develop secondary emotional problems if on medication. The diabetic in good control will avoid unnecessary conflicts, as will individuals with hypothyroidism, hyperthyroidism, or anemia.

Why art thou cast down, O my soul?
and why art thou disquieted within
me? hope thou in God: for I shall yet
praise him, who is the health of my
countenance, and my God.

PSALMS 43:5

7 Depression

The secretary came to my office door and told me there was
a patient waiting to see me. I went to the door and asked
the patient to come into my office. A lady with a sad facial
expression was sitting in a wheelchair, and her sister and
cousin were present. The sister wheeled the patient into
my office.

Discussion soon revealed that the patient wasn't sleeping nights, had no appetite, and was crying much of the
time. She had also attempted suicide the night before.

At one point in the conversation I asked, "Do you know
why you are depressed?"

"I don't know," was the answer as she burst into tears.

"How long have you been depressed?" I asked.

Her sister interrupted, "May I speak?"

"Sure," I replied.

Her sister continued, "For about the past month, she has
been very depressed."

"Did something happen a month ago?" I asked.

"No," her sister answered.

The patient appeared psychotically depressed so I
asked, "Have you been hearing voices lately?"

"Yes, I keep hearing 'Jesus Loves Me.'"

"The song, you mean," I said.

"Yes," she answered.

Her cousin commented, "She was saved recently and has been feeling guilty for all her past sins."

"I wonder if my conversion was real," the patient stated.

Realizing the patient was a suicide risk and also that she was psychotic and inclined to hallucinate, I told the patient I would like to see her when she got out of the hospital, but that for now, she should enter the hospital.

Another case and the subsequent discussion that recently transpired in my office was similar to the above, and I present it because it illustrates typical symptoms of depression. [1-5] These symptoms have been summarized under five headings. [6] All five are not always present. The number of the five that are present depends on the severity of the depression.

Five Symptoms

Sad Affect

The depressed counselee looks depressed. His face has a dejected and discouraged appearance. His forehead is furrowed and the corners of his mouth are turned down. He either cries often or feels like it. If the depression becomes severe, the depressed individual begins to look unkempt. Men stop shaving. Women stop putting on makeup. Some depressives try to hide the depression with a smile, but the depression still shows. They have what is known as a "smiling depression."

CASE 46:   Mrs. Z. denied feelings of depression. She was not crying and did not show many of the overt signs of depression. However, her face had the look of depression. Subsequent therapy sessions revealed that she did have masked depression.

Painful Thinking

As surely as organic pain hurts physically, so does emotional pain hurt mentally. The depressive feels worthless, useless, sad, helpless, and hopeless. In fact, seventy-five percent of depressives feel they will never get better (they do not know that even without medication the depression will leave in about six months).[7]

Not only may true guilt be present, but false guilt is often present to a significant degree. The depressive feels guilty for all sorts of mistakes—wrongs of the past as well as those of the present. He bears a constant haunting guilt which he cannot escape. He feels responsible for events which are realistically outside his control. For some depressives, this may have as its genesis man's need to feel important.[8] The depressive feels like a nothing, like a zero. However, he cannot be a nothing, he cannot be a zero if so much hinges on him, if he is responsible for so much. Thus, as his feelings of worthlessness grow, so does the false guilt.

As the painful thinking continues, the depressive begins to withdraw. He loses his motivation. He develops a lack of interest in activities in which he was previously involved. He becomes apathetic. He begins to lose his sense of humor. The future looks dim, and he eventually begins to feel that life is just not worth living. This leads to thoughts of suicide which then develop into plans and attempts at suicide. The depressive has been described as being self-possessed.[9] He is introspective and introverted. He is absorbed in melancholic and pessimistic thoughts. He feels he is inadequate or inferior in qualities which he feels are important, whether these qualities are intelligence, popularity, or spiritual maturity.

CASE 47: Mr. Q. presented with much guilt. He felt guilty for many minor events. He would even feel guilty for failing to smile at someone and would call to apologize for it. His behavior patterns throughout life illustrate the type of individual who is prone to false guilt and depression. Such individuals are too conscientious, too concerned, too dutiful, and unable to relax. They are too serious and their conscience is too strong—it needs reeducating according to the Word of God. Such depressive counselees need to know more about God's grace, mercy, and love.

CASE 48:   Mr. M. came to see me because he said he felt depressed. He felt blue and sad and cried often. He was sleeping poorly and had had thoughts of suicide. He was in a job that demanded much in the area of responsibility and he felt, inadequate. He, too, during the course of the therapy, was able to deal with his depression, and the symptoms disappeared. When he was initially seen in therapy, he felt downhearted, blue, and sad most of the time. He said that morning was the worst part of the day. At times he cried. He had lost weight and felt tired for no reason. His heart was beating rapidly much of the time. His mind did not seem as clear as it used to, and he found it difficult to do things that he used to be able to do. He felt restless, couldn't keep still, and did not feel hopeful about the future. He was more irritable than usual and also had difficulty making decisions. Mr. M. did not feel useful and needed and felt that his life was not full. He not only did not enjoy the things he used to do, but felt that others would be better off if he were dead. As stated previously, during the course of therapy, most of these symptoms did reverse themselves.

Psychomotor Retardation

This refers to physical changes that occur in the body with depression, the most common of which is early morning awakening. The patient awakens in the early morning hours and is not able to go back to sleep. The morning is the worst part of the day. Other forms of sleep disturbance include difficulty falling asleep or sleeping too much. In addition, there may be a disturbance in the patient's appetite so that he eats too much or too little. Thus, he may gain or lose weight. Other physiological changes occur also. For example, a tension headache, a rapid heart rate, menstrual irregularities, or gastrointestinal disturbances may be present. Diarrhea or constipation may be present. In addition, the sex drive may be lessened. Not only is the sex drive lessened, but all body acitivity may be decreased and slowed. His heart rate and rate of respiration may decelerate.

CASE 49:   Mrs. D. was referred to me from a Christian counseling center because of severe depression. She had been markedly depressed for the last several months. She had trouble both with her sleep and her appetite and had lost about twelve pounds of weight. She suffered from constipation. She had a rapid heartbeat at times, had low energy levels, and was tired for no apparent reason. During the course of the therapy Mrs. D.'s somatic complaints began to clear.

Anxiety or Agitation

Anxiety often accompanies depression. The patient may not only feel depressed but also tense. He has difficulty sitting still. He is more irritable than usual.

CASE 50:   Mrs. N. asked me several times as she was presenting her story to forgive her for being so anxious and upset. She was very depressed and having much difficulty controlling her anxiety as she presented her story. She seemed irritable and even hostile. I assured her that I understood her feelings of anxiety.

Delusional Thinking

Delusional thinking differs from painful thinking only in degree. In delusional thinking the patient may imagine things that are clearly opposed to evidence, or he may hear voices.

Widespread Occurrence of Depression

Depression is the most common symptom seen by counselors. About 8 percent of men and 16 percent of women will have a significant problem with depression during their lives.[10] It occurs twice as often in females as males.[11] It also occurs three times more often in higher socioeconomic groups.[12] About 15 percent of depressives will commit suicide, and suicide is the tenth leading cause of death in America.[13,14]

A Word About Suicide

Since depression is a leading cause of suicide, a few comments about suicide are relevant. Suicide is the tenth leading cause of death in the United States and accounts for 24,000 deaths annually. It occurs about once every twenty minutes, and there are ten unsuccessful attempts to every fatal one. In the world as a whole, the suicide rate seems to be increasing, with 500,000 cases being reported annually. Suicide is higher among the divorced, widowed, and the higher socioeconomic groups. Suicide attempts occur five times more frequently among women than men. Suicide also occurs more often in Protestants than in any other religious group. In the college-age student, it ranks second only to accidents as a cause of death.[15] Danger signals include such things as a suicide note, social isolation, a previous attempt, and, of course, depressive symptoms such as guilt, feelings of worthlessness, and an intense wish for punishment and withdrawal.

Only seven suicides are listed in the Scriptures. None of the men who committed suicide were in the will of God. Some of them previously had been but, of course, were not at the time of their death. The seven suicides are: Abimelech, recorded in Judges 9:54; Samson, recorded in Judges 16:30; Saul, recorded in 1 Samuel 31:4; Saul's armour bearer, recorded in 1 Samuel 31:5; Ahithophel, recorded in 2 Samuel 17:23; Zimri, recorded in 1 Kings 16:18; and Judas, recorded in the Gospels.

Authors have written about depression from centuries past to the present. They have noted it ranges from mild discouragement to psychotic proportions. Symptoms ranging from feeling a little low to those producing suicide have been noted. Causes ranging from physical etiologies to those produced by guilt have been noted.

Eleven Causes of Depression

Physical

An often-occurring physical problem that results in psychological discouragement is not an entity that is spectacular or profound but it is rather a simple overextension of one's self with worry. Elijah, a great man of God, is a prime example of this. In the book of 1 Kings is recorded the story of Elijah winning spiritual victories for the Lord and then plunging into discouragement. The discouragement had been preceded by his being under mental stress and probably being physically tired. Although the emotional aspects of loneliness and fear were no doubt important in the development of Elijah's discouragement, the physical factors cannot be ignored. The Lord gave Elijah food, rest, and guidance. Upon receiving these, he began to recover. Of course, Elijah had more problems than just being physically tired, but I believe this was a factor.

We, like Elijah, are prone to discouragement when we are under mental stress or are physically tired. Because of the importance of rest and nutrition, these parameters are monitored closely on a psychiatric unit. Many of one's own problems can be handled much more effectively simply by getting a good night's sleep.

Metabolic

Individuals with certain physical diseases are also more prone to depression. For example, metabolic problems such as thyroid disease and diabetes mellitus are pertinent here. For this reason, a general physical examination is in order when an individual presents with depression. With proper medication, the impact of the depression may lift.

True Guilt

Guilt may be responsible for depression. For instance, Judas felt such guilt that he committed suicide (*see* Matthew 27:5). King David also experienced much guilt and depression because of his sin with Bathsheba (*see* Psalms 32 and 51). Quoting King David, "When I kept silent *about my sin*, my body wasted away Through my groaning all day long" (Psalms 32:3 NAS). However, in contrast to Judas, David handled his guilt in a healthy manner.

Guilt may be experienced because of a sin against God or man. In the Book of Acts, for example, the Apostle Paul recorded the following, "And herein do I exercise myself, to have always a conscience void of offence toward God, and toward men" (Acts 24:16).

If the sin is against God, the solution is simple. In brief, the answer is recorded in 1 John 1:9. Quoting the Apostle John, "If we confess [agree with God about] our sins, he is faithful and just to forgive us our sins, and to cleanse us from all unrighteousness." Once an individual asks God to forgive him for a sin, God forgives and remembers the sin no more. The individual may still feel guilty if he has not thoroughly learned of the mercy of God, but this guilt is not of God.

Although all sins are against God, some also affect people, and although God completely forgives the sin, an obligation exists toward a person offended. The love of Christ constrains us to ask forgiveness of those we have offended. However, I do not believe one should search in the past for possible sins and individuals he has offended, but rather that if the Holy Spirit continues to convict of a particular offense, the issue should be settled. The apology should not contain unnecessary and embarrassing details, and it should be only to the one offended. Finally, in apologizing when one is only partially at fault, he will be more effective if he uses wording that places the responsibility upon himself rather than both himself and the other person. Otherwise the other individual will become defensive, and the purpose of the apology will be defeated.

False Guilt

Christians with obsessive-compulsive personalities will be prone to depression. An obsessive-compulsive personality type has been well-documented by observation to be a specific personality pattern. This personality is characterized by being overly rigid, conscientious, and perfectionistic. Moreover, this type of person is absorbed in right and wrong. And being overly dutiful, he is unable to relax or have fun. To be sure, his conscience is stricter than God Himself. Whereas in sociopaths the conscience is underdeveloped, in obsessive-compulsive individuals the conscience is overdeveloped. In either case, the issue is not so much what the individual thinks, but what the Word of God says. An obsessive-compulsive individual needs to educate himself repeatedly concerning the grace and mercy of God. Rather than being absorbed in the letter of the law, he would benefit from the thought expressed by Christ in the following words, " . . . the words that I speak unto you, they are spirit, and they are life" (John 6:63). He needs to relax and enjoy part of the abundant life that God desires for him (*see* John 10:10). And concerning his numerous worries, the advice of Apostle Paul is applicable:

> Finally, brethren, whatsoever things are true, whatsoever things are honest, whatsoever things are just, whatsoever things are pure, whatsoever things are lovely, whatsoever things are of good report; if there be any virtue, and if there be any praise, think on these things.
>
> PHILIPPIANS 4:8

Misplaced Guilt

Whether true, false, or misplaced, it is feasible that any emotionally drained individual may feel guilty for some sin in the past and displace guilt to numerous insigificant areas.

Anger Turned Inward

Depression has been defined as anger turned inward. This anger may be the result of the loss of a love object. This love object varies from a loved one to self-esteem. If the loved object is another person, the patient becomes very angry with the individual, but then turns the anger toward himself, and thus becomes depressed. The anger may also be the result of the violation of one's "rights."[16]

In either case, bitterness and then depression result. Thus, if a Christian is wronged, what should he do? If he holds his anger in and becomes bitter, he runs the risk of depression. Anger can often be expressed in an appropriate way verbally, and a better and closer relationship develops between persons. Often a person needs to be more assertive. This is especially true in depressed people. Yet, he does not believe in letting his anger show at the expense of hurting others unnecessarily. The following are helpful steps:

- Realize that there may be bitterness toward another or others.
- List those who have offended.
- Forgive them because of the love of Christ (*see* Matthew 6:12), and because depression is too high a price to pay.
- Give up "rights" (*see* Philippians 3:7). Since depression may be anger turned inward, and since anger usually results from a violation of what one considers to be his rights, one solution for bitterness is to give up one's "rights" to God. One day I did this. The question I essentially asked myself was, "Who is smarter, God or I?"

Christians often consider time, their cars, their health, etc., to be "rights." However, God desires to give these back to us as privileges. If one has no rights, they cannot be violated, and one cannot thus become angry. Of course, because of the tendency to reclaim privileges as rights, this yielding is not a one-time occasion.

- Talk it out. I do not believe in expressing anger at the expense of hurting others unnecessarily. However, often others need things pointed out to them. Sitting down and talking with another in an appropriate manner (*see* Galatians 6:1) can be very helpful for both, and helps to externalize rather than internalize the anger.

- Express emotionally charged energy in exercise. This gives one the opportunity to express and release pent-up energy. It also allows time to become more objective.

Self-Effort

A major reason for discouragement among dedicated Christians is their trying to live and work for Christ in their own strength. Clearly, the Christian life is a supernatural life and can only be lived through the power of the Holy Spirit. Thus, Apostle Paul stated, "I can do all things through Christ . . . " (Philippians 4:13) and again he stated, " . . . it is God which worketh in you both to will and to do of his good pleasure" (Philippians 2:13). In contrast, in Romans 7:24, he recorded his discouragement that resulted from trying to live for God in his own energy.

If the Lord has a ministry He wants accomplished, and if an individual is available, God will accomplish what He desires. To be sure, wrong priorities and assuming responsibilities (even in Christian activities) beyond what God desires is a major cause of discouragement. God is mostly concerned with an individual's really getting to know Him (*see* Philippians 3:10 AMPLIFIED); secondly, with his meeting the needs of his family (*see* 1 Timothy 5:8); and thirdly, with ministering to others in the particular ways God has chosen for him.

Wrong Perspective

In Psalms 73 is recorded the discouragement and depression that came to King David as a result of a wrong perspective.[17]

Quoting King David, "But as for me, my feet were almost gone; my steps had well nigh slipped. For I was envious at the foolish, when I saw the prosperity of the wicked" (*see* Psalms 73:2–3).

Likewise, many things that God has not chosen to give

an individual today may appear very inviting to him. He may forget the only two tangible things that are going to last—the Word of God and people (*see* Matthew 24:35 and 1 John 4:11–12). These are the things that are really important. He may temporarily forget that the inner love, joy, and peace he wants are the results of the fruit of the Spirit (*see* Galatians 5:22–23), and not material or wordly things.

In verses 16 and 17 of Chapter 73 of Psalms, King David recorded the moment that suddenly his perspective changed. He stated, "When I thought to know this, it was too painful for me; Until I went into the sanctuary of God; then understood I their end." This sanctuary for each Christian today may be different. It may be getting away to relax. It may be memorizing some particular verses. It may be having more fellowship with Christians. It may be getting out and sharing Christ with others.

King Solomon's conclusion after seeking fulfillment in life from humanitarianism, sex, amusement, education, and pleasure was " . . . vanity of vanities; all is vanity" (Ecclesiastes 1:2). That statement sounds like an answer from a modern day, depressed patient. Solomon's record of his search for fulfillment is found in two books in the Bible which are back-to-back[18]. One is Ecclesiastes, in which Solomon records his search by means described in sources above. The second book is Song of Solomon. This book is an analogy of a human love relationship to Christ and His Church. If we carry the logic, the analogy represents the relationship found in a well-balanced life of Bible study, prayer, fellowship, and witnessing. This perspective is found only through an intimate, cultivated fellowship with Christ Himself.

Adjustment Reactions

I have often used the diagnosis of *adjustment reaction* in psychiatry to describe a particularly stressful time in life for any given individual.

One major category of depression has been called

exogenous depression, which means that the depression comes from without rather than within the individual. The individual is reacting to external stress. There is nothing abnormal about feeling acutely stressed or down at times, although it is detrimental to remain that way. There is nothing wrong with being perplexed (*see* 2 Corinthians 4:8–9), but it is wrong to carry this to despair. Being perplexed drives us to Christ, but remaining in despair results in depression.

Attacks by Satan

When one feels discouraged or uncomfortable, how can he be sure God is not trying to tell him something? While attending a Navigator's Christian conference, I was exposed to the following points that are helpful:[19]

GOD	*SATAN or Possibly SELF*
a. The individual can identify a specific problem accounting for his discouragement. However, caution should be used because this is not necessarily from God.	a. The reason for discouragement may remain vague. Confusion is a prominent feature, and God is not the author of confusion (*see* 1 Corinthians 14:33).
b. The individual senses there is hope.	b. The individual feels hopeless.
c. The person senses he can be built up through dealing with his problems.	c. The person feels downgraded.

A Learned Response

Although there is no current diagnosis of depressive personality, it seems there are many people who are just habitually depressed. In some families the children are indirectly taught that the appropriate way to handle stress is to become depressed. Depression is acceptable in these families. Several members in the family may suffer from depression. Depression becomes a learned response. These individuals go through life depressed, and depression seems to have become a part of their personalities. In these individuals depression may become a powerful tool by which to manipulate others. Thus, a young child may learn to get attention when he is depressed, and the learned response is reinforced.

Endogenous Depression

One way depression has been categorized is by describing it as *endogenous* or *exogenous*. As stated previously, the exogenous depression is caused by a person's reaction to external stress. On the other hand, endogenous depression comes totally from within the individual. Exogenous depression has been a favorite subject of psychiatric articles through the years.[20]

The foundation for exogenous depression could start very early in life. During the interview, the counselor often notes a history of a cold, rejecting mother. The baby felt rejected. In fact, he started to expect everyone to reject him just as his mother did. This expectation of rejection led to feelings of hostility. To avoid getting close to others and thus avoid being rejected, the patient started projecting his hostile feelings onto others and imagining they did not want to get to know him. He is hostile toward others but imagines they are hostile toward him. He does not want to become close to others but imagines they do not want to be close to him. The avoidance of being close to anyone left the patient with a host of unmet dependency needs. To compensate for these needs, the depressive may become superindependent. He may become a superman-independent, a friend to all who need help.

If one examines the above, he can see that a cycle has been set up. The cycle alternates between feelings of rejection, unmet dependency needs, hostility, projection of the hostility, and avoidance of close relationships. The following story has been told to illustrate the cycle.

A depressive is driving down a country road and has a flat tire. He looks in his trunk for a jack. Not finding one he spots a farm house one-quarter mile away with a truck in the front yard and says to himself, "I'll go borrow his jack." As he approaches the house he is feeling bad (1) for failing to have a jack, (2) for having to depend on someone else for help. As he gets nearer the farm house he begins to expect rejection and to get angry over what is his expectation of rejection. He becomes more and more angry at unmet dependency needs (projects the anger he feels toward himself for needing the jack), so that by the time he knocks on the door, the farmer opens the door and the depressive yells, "Keep your jack." This will usually guarantee that he doesn't get the jack and he walks back re-convinced that you can't depend on people.[21]

The patient can really benefit from insights into these behavior patterns. He can learn that *he can change rejection* by others by changing his rejections of them. He can learn he does have dependency needs and how to *meet those dependency needs* in appropriate ways. He can begin to learn that no one can be a superman, and *no one is perfect*. He can begin to *recognize his feelings* and begin to deal with them and his anger more appropriately. He can recognize that although these behavior patterns may have started in early life, *he can change them*.

Other Causes

There are several other causes of depression. For example, postpartum depression seems to be in a category of its own. This depression following the birth of a child is not uncommon. Another depression that seems to be in a category of its own is the depression seen during adolescence. This depression is especially different in that the symptoms are often different from the symptoms seen in adults. Rather than having a sad facial expression and crying often, the adolescent starts to "act out" socially. He may steal, lie, or "act out" sexually.

Mention should also be made of problems that simulate

depression but are not depression itself. For example, grief is not depression. It is grief and is very normal. Also, certain personality types such as hysterics, will present with the chief complaint of depression. Further evaluation may reveal this to be more a presenting complaint rather than the real problem.

Nine Ways of Dealing with Depression

In addition to the specific causes of depression listed previously, the following nine factors are helpful in dealing with depression:

Medication. Antidepressive medication doses produce significant improvement in mood, sleep, and appetite, and thus the individual is better able to deal with his problems. In depression there may be an actual chemical abnormality, and antidepressive medication corrects this abnormality. In addition, it works in other ways to improve mood, sleep, and appetite.

For example, antidepressants (*tricyclics*) have effects on the following systems:[22]

- Limbic structures. The effect here results in improved mood.
- Hypothalamus. The effect here results in improved appetite and other biologic functions.
- Reticular activating system (inhibited). The effect here results in improved sleep.
- Neurohumoral deposits. These are increased with medication, and this may account for much of the beneficial effects.

Christian counselors have, at times, been opposed to drugs used to improve the mood. I believe an examination of how the drug works is important in considering the validity of the drug used. If the drug corrects an actual biochemical abnormality and returns the body back to its usual physiologic state, I believe the use is valid. For example, who would argue with the use of insulin to return a diabetic to a normal physiologic state? In like manner, some drugs used in psychiatry serve simply to return the body back to a balanced physiologic state. For example, the antidepressive medications (tricyclics) build norepinephrine, a neurotransmitter in the brain which is important in returning the emotional state back to a normal level. The tricyclics simply block the re-uptake of norepinephrine at the nerve endings, thereby increasing the norepinephrine in the synapse between the nerve cells. When this level becomes normal, much of the depression disappears. Of course, the basic problems must still be dealt with in order to really help the patient.

On the other hand, if the drugs do not correct an abnormal physiologic state, I question their validity. For example, amphetamines give an artificial lift to mood. However, they do not restore the body to a balanced physiologic state, and in a couple of weeks, the depression returns stronger than ever.

A friend. A warm and understanding friend who will listen is of great help to a depressed person. Often the depressed patient has a low self-esteem. In this case, a friend can help the individual to have a sane estimate of himself (*see* Romans 12:3). This is done not by just telling him that he is important, but by proving it to him by actions that show interest in him.

A focus on behavior. If there is no apparent cause for the depression, the depressed person should focus on daily planned activities, avoiding those activities that would tend to produce more depression, and practicing activities that are priority. For example, the following are practical suggestions:

- Avoid soap operas
- Get up early
- Go to work regardless of feelings
- Have sufficient times with family
- Do something nice for your mate
- Have time of enjoyment with others

In other words, focus on behavior, not just feelings. It is important to let the counselee ventilate and talk out his feelings; this helps to deal with the internalized anger that has caused the depression, and helps to bring the anxiety from the subconscious (where it cannot be dealt with appropriately) to the conscious. This also helps the counselee to feel the counselor cares for him and understands him. However, the counselor must move beyond just dealing with feelings and also deal with behavior. Indeed, we have little direct control over our feelings, but maximum control over our behavior.[23] The patient will benefit by developing new interests and activities. The Bible acknowledges that feelings are important (*see* Hebrews 4:15) but it also puts a great emphasis on the importance of behavior whereas *behavior* is mentioned much[24]. (*See* Philippians 4:13; 2:13; James 1:22; Genesis 4:6–7.)

Prayer.   Verbally expressing troubles in prayer is helpful. King David said that morning, noon, and night, he would pray and cry *aloud*. Just ventilating alone would help, but how much more helpful it is to share with God who has the power to give a " . . . sound mind" (*see* 2 Timothy 1:7).

Word.   The Word of God gives joy to counteract depression. Thus Jeremiah said, "Thy words were found, and I did eat them; and thy word was unto me the joy and rejoicing of mine heart: for I am called by thy name, O Lord God of hosts" (Jeremiah 15:16). To be sure, the Word of God is " . . . quick, and powerful . . . " (Hebrews 4:12).

Fellowship.   If one is around other Christians with joy, he will catch it. Solomon stated, "Iron sharpeneth iron; so a man sharpeneth the countenance of his friend" (Proverbs 27:17).

Focus on a plan.   In particularly stressful situations that are producing discouragement, formulate a plan of action.[25] List all alternatives of what to do, and then try the one chosen.

Focus on assertiveness.   The depressed patient is often very unassertive. In fact, he can hardly say *no* to anyone when asked to do something. If the patient can become healthily assertive, he will probably improve. It is helpful to encourage the patient to say *no* when what he is requested to do is not on his priority list (God, family, joy, ministry), and is not really helpful to the other person. Likewise, if the patient can appropriately express his feelings, he will probably improve. Rather than being too assertive, the depressed person has often gone to the other extreme and does not speak up when he should.

Insight.   Insight is very important. It has been dealt with previously.

Favour is deceitful, and beauty is vain: but a woman that feareth the Lord, she shall be praised.

PROVERBS 31:30

8 The Sensuous Woman and the Sociopathic Man

A Psychiatric Survey

During my residency in psychiatry, I did a categorical survey of the types of patients I had during a six-month rotation on the psychiatric ward. These findings were obtained:

- 30%—Hysterical trends, personality or neurosis
- 20%—Depression/anxiety
- 10%—Drug-related problems
- 15%—Psychotic

The patients also revealed the following:

- 60%—females (40 percent males)
- The most frequent age was 20–35 years. The number of teenagers and individuals over fifty was also significant.
- The overwhelming majority of patients indicated they wanted help very much.
- Most had some type of religious training, and a significant number were Christians.

144

Conclusions are difficult to draw from such a small sample of a patient population (approximately 40), but one can conclude with certainty that individuals with emotional conflicts are in search of help. One may also conclude that being a Christian does not necessarily free one of emotional turmoil.

In my particular survey, I found *hysteria* was the most common problem. This certainly does not document that this is the main emotional problem today, but judging from other observations, it does seem to be a prevalent problem if we use the term in a broad sense. Solomon probably dealt with the sensuous woman more than any other single issue, which again documents the importance and magnitude of the problem.

One characteristic of an hysterical personality is that of being seductive. However, it should be pointed out that although the hysterical personality is often seductive, the reverse is not always true. All sensuous women are not hysterical.

Our society is increasingly focusing on the sensuous woman. Thus, many advertisements are based on sexual appeals as are many movies. The irony of the situation is that although the sensuous woman is presented as outwardly inviting and warm, she is inwardly lonely and frustrated. Hence, she appears as a great sex partner, but in reality she often never reaches a climax or orgasm. She may appear as loving, but inside she feels bitterness which prevents a warm loving relationship with free sexual expression. She desires love and affection, and thus by seductive dress and actions she attempts to obtain these, but the close interaction she seeks is blocked by her subconscious fears.

If Christian girls have these trends and do not find God's answers, they will live frustrated lives. Likewise, if Christian men marry girls with these traits, they too will live disappointed lives unless they know how to deal with their problems and values.

Psychiatric Examples

The following summarizes common features in patients with hysterical trends:

1. Mrs. S. presented with the chief complaint that she was depressed. She had been treated by a couple of psychiatrists in the past for depression, but it was becoming worse.

Comment: These women may seem depressed, and sympathetic counselors may be manipulated by this. However, depression is only the surface and not the root problem. Recognizing this in this particular lady and applying some other principles, I was able to help her. These principles are shared later.

2. Mrs. J. presented to the psychiatric unit because of a suicidal gesture.

Comment: There is often a history of several rather feeble suicide gestures. These are usually manipulative in nature. In fact, although men are twice as apt to die by suicide, women attempt suicide five times more.

3. Mrs. T. had been married several times and her present marriage was unstable.

Comment: These women seem to repeatedly find an idealized male, marry him, become disappointed, and then divorce him.

To account for this, the psychoanalytic school has proposed the following theory: The idealized male represents the patient's father. Disappointment comes because the male turns out not to be perfect, just as the father. Ambivalence for men is reinforced. Hence, unresolved conflicts between father and daughter still cause problems. Disappointment comes because of deep-seated bitterness the patient has toward her father and thus, toward men in general.

4. Mrs. A. was seductive in her dress and actions.

Comment: This partially results because the girl wants to be accepted and loved, as commented before. One possible reason for her being seductive is having learned as a young child that she could gain attention from her father by such behavior. This pattern was continued in relationships with other men.

5. Mrs. M. tended to be dramatic, vain, excitable, emotionally unstable, and immature. At one time in her life, she had been close to the Lord and had been happy. During one interview I shared the following:

"You apparently have a real need for someone to care for you, and there is someone who wants to know you more than you want to know him."

"Who?" she asked.

"Christ," I answered.

She agreed and we proceeded to outline her responsibilities and a plan that could aid in reestablishing a true inward peace.

It should be pointed out that men may also have hysterical personalities. Possibly men are diagnosed less often for this for several reasons. First, Greeks set the trend of diagnosing only women with this problem when they said it was due to a migrating uterus and therefore applied only to women. Secondly, men are usually the ones who make the diagnosis, and they may be biased in their conclusions. Thirdly, a male with these characteristics (manipulative, self-centered, feeling little guilt, etc.) might be commonly diagnosed as *sociopathic* rather than *hysterical*.

Therapy of the Sensuous Woman

Therapy is dealt with in later chapters, but briefly, I have three points I use in therapy with an hysteric.

First, one must consider the need for medication. Of

course, there is no medication for immaturity. However, hysterics can become very depressed or anxious. Some depression and anxiety can be helpful because it motivates a person to change, but if the depression is extreme, one runs the risk of suicide, and antidepressive medication should be considered.

Secondly, the counselor must consider what type of approach and attitude he will use. In general, the counselor wants to be warm and friendly. However, since hysterics may misinterpret this, and since they are very manipulative, an adult-to-adult or matter-of-fact approach proves best.

Thirdly, in counseling sessions the counselor should use a reality-oriented type of approach. The patient needs to look at her behavior in reality. For example, does she realize she is being seductive? What is she willing to do about it? This patient concentrates on feelings and neglects logic. She needs to be encouraged to think about what she is doing, to think logically and rationally, and to think more and feel less. I have found it helpful to confront the patient with her irresponsible behavior and then help her plan appropriate behavior and methods to deal with specific problems.

I find it very interesting to compare current psychiatric views of the hysterical personality with those of the Bible concerning the seductive woman. This illustrates that the Bible is as modern and relevant today as it was in the early Church. I should mention that in the following descriptions only a general comparison can be made. The psychiatric description is only of the personality type having the prominent characteristic of being seductive or sensuous. The psychiatric diagnosis does not necessarily pertain, in and of itself, to all sensuous women. The following is taken from *Diagnostic and Statistical Manual of Mental Disorders* and other studies in psychiatry.

The Sensuous Woman
The Bible and Psychiatry Compared

Psychiatry	Bible
1. She is manipulative.	1. She "... flatters with her words ..." (Proverbs 2:16 NAS). "... smoother than oil is her speech ..." (Proverbs 5:3 NAS).
2. She may be characterized by a series of marriages and divorces.	2. She "... leaves the companion of her youth ..." (Proverbs 2:17 NAS).
3. She does not think. When working with this type of personality, psychiatrists are taught to help the patient to think because she goes through life feeling much but really thinking little.	3. "She does not ponder the path of life ..." (Proverbs 5:6 NAS).
4. She is emotionally unstable.	4. "... her ways are unstable ..." (Proverbs 5:6 NAS).
5. She is vain and self-centered.	5. She is outwardly beautiful but inwardly vain and self-centered (Proverbs 6:25, 7:10–21 NAS).
6. She is seductive.	6. She is seductive in both dress and actions (*see* Proverbs 7:10–21 NAS). "... she seduces him" (Proverbs 7:21 NAS). "... catch you with her eyelids" (Proverbs 6:25 NAS). "... dressed as a harlot ..." (Proverbs 7:10 NAS).
7. She is dependent on others. She uses the defense of rationalization.	7. She rationalizes in her mind for her impurity. She feels no guilt (*see* Proverbs 30:20 NAS).

Psychiatry	Bible
8. Her basic motivation is hatred. Psychoanalysis in effect teaches that the basic motivation behind the hysterical woman is hatred for men.	8. She desires the downfall of her lover. "... many are the victims she has cast down ..." (Proverbs 7:26 NAS).
9. She is overreactive and dramatic.	9. "She is boisterous and rebellious ..." (Proverbs 7:11 NAS).
10. She is naive. Although outwardly seductive and a woman of the world, she is basically very naive and really is often sexually frigid.	10. "She is naive ... (Proverbs 9:13 NAS).
11. She is attention seeking.	11. She is attention seeking (*see* Proverbs 7:10–21 NAS). NAS).
12. Prognosis poor.	12. Prognosis is poor (*see* Proverbs 2:18). But there is reason to be optimistic, and there is hope (*see* account of Jesus and the woman of Sychar in John 4).

The Sociopathic Man

The counterpart of the hysterical woman is the sociopathic man. It seems to me that if psychiatrists see certain traits in a woman, they tend to diagnose her as hysterical, whereas if they see similar traits in a man, they tend to diagnose him as sociopathic. As in an hysterical personality, the sociopathic personality is characterized by being self-centered and immature. He is out for himself and in fact, seldom forms close personal relations with anyone.

In the survey listed at the beginning of this chapter, I noted that 10 percent of those patients had an alcohol or drug-related problem. A significant percent of them had sociopathic traits. And this is in keeping with *sociopathy,* for often sociopaths do have an alcohol or drug-related problem. As stated earlier, these individuals are characterized by a lack of conscience. They do not feel guilt for wrongdoings. They do not seem to learn from experience. Yet, they are charming and likeable, having traits which facilitate an ability to manipulate people. They feel they are OK and the rest of the world is NOT OK.

PSYCHIATRY	BIBLE: ROMANS 1
1. Repeated conflict with society	Murder, deceit, disobedient to parents
2. Incapable of loyalty to others	Full of envy, spiteful, covenant breakers, backbiters
3. Selfish	Covetous, full of envy, proud boasters
4. Callous	Filled with unrighteousness
5. Not able to learn from experience	Without understanding

Therapy of the Sociopathic Man

First, a comment about medicine would be helpful. A sociopath, as anyone else, can become anxious or depressed, but the therapist would be especially careful about giving this individual any medicine because of his tendency to abuse drugs. In fact, he often comes into therapy with the ulterior motive of obtaining drugs.

Secondly, the counselor must again consider what type of attitude will work best. Usually, a matter-of-fact or confrontational approach works best.

Thirdly, the counselor must consider whether he is willing to work with this individual. I have heard psychiatrists cynically commenting on the undependability of sociopaths, "Diagnose them and then discharge them."

As Christians, we have more hope. Sociopaths can become Christians. They can understand the gospel and put their faith in Christ. I believe this is their main hope. I should also mention that many of them will improve with age, for they seem to "burn out," or expend the energy they devote to themselves.

Part III

Treating Emotional Problems

To everything there is a season, and a time to every purpose under the heaven ... a time to keep silence, and a time to speak.

ECCLESIASTES 3:1, 7

9 Indirect-Directive Counseling

Principles in Counseling

Christian counseling is many faceted, but basically the principles can be put into three broad categories. The first category has to do with the counselor's relationship to Jesus Christ. As in any work for God, we are only the instruments through which God works, and the real effectiveness of the work depends on God. The second category has to do with certain attributes the counselor needs to become involved in a meaningful way with the patient. It involves really caring for the patient. This is what patients want to find. Caring is something patients can sense, and the relationship that develops because of this is of paramount importance in helping the patient. Thus, more important than the type of counseling used is the personality of the counselor. Lastly, the third category has to do with the type of counseling approach used. I have found an *indirect-directive* type of approach the most effective. This is the topic of this chapter. The other two categories will be discussed later.

Directive Versus Non-Directive Counseling

Counseling breaks down into two broad divisions: *directive* and *non-directive* as the therapies of William Glasser and Carl Rogers illustrate. Without a doubt, men through the years have lost balance in extremes in one direction or the other. Psychiatrists in the past have been criticized for being non-directive, and I agree. Yet, I fear some Christian counselors have erred in being too directive rather than helping an individual form a value judgment for himself.

If a counselor is too non-directive he is not fair to the counselee. Counselees consult others whom they feel have wisdom and can guide them in an appropriate direction. The counselor owes the patient this.

If a counselor is too directive, however, he defeats his own purpose. Only if a decision is a personal conviction, will it last. The following example illustrates the point:

I recall a case in which one Christian friend was telling another Christian friend that he was definitely living in the wrong location, and that he should move to an area where God wanted him to be. The counselor giving the advice was very dogmatic, perhaps made his friend defensive, and apparently did not succeed in helping him develop his own value judgment. While the counselor giving the advice may have been very correct in his thinking, his method proved insufficient.

I do not wish to discredit the importance of being direct when indicated. In fact, Christ was often very direct, as were Elihu, Solomon, and Apostle Paul. Christ was directive at times and non-directive at other times. In Matthew 13 is recorded an instance when He taught the people in parables and thus was less than overtly directive (*see* Matthew 13:3). However, in Matthew 19 is recorded an instance when he was very directive with a rich young man (*see* Matthew 19:21–23). The point is that each individual must be dealt with as an individual, and the approach must be tailored. For example, hysterics respond best to directive counseling, but obsessive-compulsive patients often respond best to non-directive techniques. In either case, the value judgment can only be made by the counselee.

It should be noted that I have used the term "indirect" rather than "non-direct." Technically, they are not the same, and I am referring to direct and indirect counseling rather than direct and non-direct counseling. However, I doubt that any therapist is ever truly non-directive for we are directive with every move we make.

In brief, the approach I have found the most effective is an *indirect-directive* approach. The approach is directive in that the counselor should know what the counselee needs to do to handle his problems and how to guide him in that direction. The counselor should be able to recognize the problem and approach it accordingly. Also, because the Bible is the Christian counselor's standard of authority, his counseling is directive. His goals are to help the counselee solve his problems in accordance with the Will of God and to help the counselee grow spiritually. Inasmuch as the Bible is the counselor's foundation and guide, his counseling is directive.

The approach is indirect in that the counselor often uses indirect techniques (questions, suggestive statements, listening) to help the counselee reach appropriate decisions. The counselor uses *indirect* techniques for a *directed* end. If a decision is a counselee's own, it will be much more meaningful and lasting.

In the Book of 2 Samuel is recorded an instance in which Nathan, a prophet of God, used this method. King David had sinned with the wife of Uriah the Hittite. This displeased the Lord, and He sent Nathan to rebuke David. Nathan was very intelligent, and he knew the dangers of rebuking a king. Thus, he had to help the king obtain valuable insight without giving direct advice. He must have known that we often react to the shortcomings in others because they are present in ourselves. So, he proceeded to tell King David the following story and accomplished his objective. The verses which follow may be thought of as: King David on Trial.

> Then the Lord sent Nathan to David. And he came to him, and said, "There were two men in one city, the one rich and the other poor. The rich man had a great many flocks and herds. But the poor man had nothing except one little ewe lamb Which he bought and nourished; and it grew up together with him and his children. It would eat of his bread and drink of his cup and lie in his bosom, And was like a daughter to him. Now a traveler came to the rich man, And he was unwilling to take from his own flock or his own herd, To prepare for the wayfarer who had come to him; Rather he took the poor man's ewe lamb and prepared it for the one who had come to him."
> Then David's anger burned greatly against the man, and he said to Nathan, "As the Lord lives, surely the man who has done this deserves to die. And he must make restitution for the lamb fourfold, because he did this thing and had no compassion."
>
> Nathan then said to David, "You are the man! . . ."
>   2 SAMUEL 12:1–7 NAS

Christ—The Approach He Used in Counseling

Christ was a master at helping others obtain valuable insights. He did this through statements, questions, and parables. His statements were at times stern and rebuking, but at other times they were kind and gentle. Likewise, the types of questions He asked varied. The Gospel according to Mark records approximately twenty questions that were asked by Christ. Nearly half of the twenty questions were directed at either the Pharisees, the religious leaders of the day, or the multitudes. A couple of questions were directed at individuals. Most of the questions seemed matter-of-fact, and their purpose was most often to teach or help others gain insight. And while Christ was kind and loving, He remained objective, and at least five of the twenty questions (three directed at the Pharisees and two directed at the disciples) were rebuking and cutting in nature.

The Art of Asking Questions

Questions force others to think and reach their own conclusions when declarations might be disregarded. The ability to help others gain insights by questions is largely learned, and in trained hands is one of the most valuable tools a counselor has.

The Present Versus the Past—Feelings Versus Behavior

The pendulum in counseling seems to be swinging from focusing on the past to focusing on the "here and now." The pendulum also seems to be swinging from focusing on feelings to focusing on behavior.

There are two extremes of position when considering the importance of the past. One is to blame the past for present, inappropriate behavior. This extreme in counseling focuses almost entirely on the past. The other extreme tends to avoid the past entirely and counseling centers around the present only. I have found that a balanced view works best. In counseling, I focus mostly on present behavior and specific plans to deal with problems; however, I realize that unresolved issues that occurred in the past must be dealt with appropriately. I do not fail to recognize that the past forms much of an individual's personality, and although an individual is responsible for present behavior, early environmental stresses can cause an individual to be more prone to detrimental defense mechanisms. The first five years of life are a major factor in determining whether an individual will be an extrovert, introvert, leader, follower, quiet, loud, dramatic, or shy. Thus, in agreement with Reality Therapy, I focus on the present, but will deal with or listen to the past as indicated.

There are also the extremes of feelings and behavior. One school will focus entirely on feelings in counseling, the other will refuse to allow the counselee to talk about feelings that are important to him. The Bible recognizes the importance of feelings (*see* Hebrews 4:15) but it places much emphasis on behavior. We should understand our feelings but not let them rule us. The founders of Reality Therapy have well expressed the importance of behavior in their statement that one has maximum control over his behavior but minimum control over his feelings.

In summary, I would offer the following three suggestions to Christian counselors to help them offer balanced and effective care for their counselees:

Genuinely care. Caring is something that is intangible but that people can really sense. This is especially true in individuals with problems. We all gravitate to people who are warm, understanding, accepting, personal, and who will listen to us. These qualities are of utmost importance for the Christian counselor (*see* Galatians 4:19; Romans 1:11–12, John 17:19–21).

Caring results in the building of a relationship. The relationship that exists determines much of the progress of therapy. Without a relationship, a commitment from a counselee means little. Without a relationship, the counselee is often not motivated to change.

Use an indirect-directive approach. This may sound like a play on words, but I have found this approach to be the key foundation of my counseling. Again, by the term "indirect-directive," I mean that the approach is directive in the sense that the counselor knows what direction would be healthy for the one counseled and guides him in that direction. It is also directive because God's Word is the counselor's standard of authority. The approach is indirect in the sense that unless a person reaches his own decisions, he is not likely to benefit. Christ often used questions to help others reach decisions. As was mentioned earlier, approximately twenty questions are recorded that Christ asked. Open-ended questions, leading questions, and teaching questions have all been of great help to me. If a young person is told, for example, that only two things will last (God's Word and people), he might remember this for a short period. On the contrary, if he is asked what two things will last, and he comes up with the solution, this will more likely remain in his memory. Without a doubt, counselors through the years have lost balance by becoming either too indirective or too directive, and psychiatry is now catching the rebound from resentment because of a rather extreme indirect approach at times. However, Christian counselors have also been guilty at times of robbing the counselee of the benefit he could have gained in finding God's will for himself. Of course, there are many times to be directive. Discernment must be used to know which to use.

I believe the key here is *insight.* Once a counselee gains insight into the true nature of the problem much of the problem may resolve.

Help the patient formulate a specific plan of action to deal with his problem.   After I understand what a counselee's specific problems are, I help him formulate a plan of action. Although ventilating one's problems and expressing one's feelings of guilt and depression can be of much help, this alone is not enough. A specific plan of action is needed to deal with the problems and then, as problems are solved, feelings will change. Several counseling movements today (Reality Therapy, Transactional Analysis, and others) are stressing the importance of making specific plans and setting goals.

The Counseling Process

The counseling process could be understood as follows:

Let counselee *ventilate.* Listen to counselee.
$$\downarrow$$
Help the counselee gain *insight.*
$$\downarrow$$
Help counselee formulate a specific *plan of action.*

This chapter has dealt in general with treating emotional problems. Previous chapters have dealt with recognizing spiritual, psychological, and physical problems. The following is an outline for ministers and Christian counselors of the counseling process for each of these three categories. One needs to remember that spiritual and psychological problems break down into four broad subdivisions as in the following outline.

An Outline of the Treatment Measures
For Spiritual, Psychological, and Physical Problems

I. Spiritual Problems (*see* 1 Thessalonians 5:14): Use one of five types of biblical counseling
   A. A need to know Christ (*see* Romans 1:16)
      1. During the course of counseling (after a relationship has been built) ask the counselee about his religious background.
      2. Share the gospel.
      3. Write out verses on salvation (*see* Romans 3:23, Romans 6:23, John 1:12).
      4. Keep it simple.
      5. Give counselee an opportunity to believe in Christ.

   B. A need to grow in Christ (*see* 1 Peter 2:2)
      1. Do a Bible study series with the counselee on discipleship. The Bible study should focus on the basics in the Christian life (God's Word, prayer, Christian fellowship, and witnessing). Help the counselee form a solid foundation in each of these areas and thus a balanced (healthy, mature) Christian life.
      2. Have the counselee memorize three verses per week.
      3. Help the counselee figure out a specific plan for having a quiet time.

    4. Help the counselee become involved in a church. For further support help the counselee become involved with a smaller group within the church (a minichurch).

C. A need to deal with a specific sin (*see* 2 Thessalonians 3:5)
    1. Listen to the counselee and build a relationship.
    2. Confront the counselee about his sin.
    3. Ask for a one-week commitment (until the next appointment) to avoid the sin.
    4. Give the counselee a short Bible study (approximately one page) on the problem area to do prior to the next appointment. Make the focus of the Bible study on personal application.
    5. Ask the counselee to memorize three verses per week that deal with the problem.
    6. For support and strength to overcome the temptation, help the counselee to become involved with fellow Christians in a church, minichurch, or another Christian group.
    7. Ask the counselee to have a quiet time daily.

D. Demonic influences (demon possession or demon oppression)
    1. Share concepts in Ephesians 6.
    2. Point out that Satan is aware of the particular temptations one is prone to and the weaknesses he has.

II. Psychological problems
  A. Psychophysiologic problems (ulcer, colitis, high blood pressure, etc.)
    1. Counsel with the counselee concerning the spiritual and psychological aspects of his problem.

    2. Refer to the local medical doctor for treatment of the physical aspect of the problem.

    3. If needed, work with another professional concerning the psychological aspect.

B. Personality trait or personality disorder

    1. Discern the personality traits and vary your counseling approach accordingly. For example, do not approach an individual with hysterical traits the same as one with depression traits.

    2. *Listen* with empathy as counselee tells of his presenting problem, past history, and feelings.

    3. Explain to the counselee the strengths and potential weaknesses of his personality. Help him gain *insight*.

    4. Help the counselee to formulate a specific *plan of action* to deal with his problem.

    5. If needed, work with another professional who has training in psychology or psychiatry.

C. Neurosis (a biologic and social impairment)

    1. Discern the type of neurosis and approach accordingly.

    2. *Listen* with empathy as counselee tells of his presenting problem, past history, and feelings.

    3. Explain to the counselee what he is doing and what is happening to him. Help him gain *insight*.

    4. Help the counselee formulate a specific *plan of action* to deal with his problem.

    5. If needed, work with another professional who has training in psychology or psychiatry. This may be needed when a threat of suicide or homicide exists. It will also be necessary when the counselor realizes the problem is beyond his ability to handle. If medication is needed, refer to a psychiatrist. If psychological tests are needed, refer to a psychologist. Of course, either can do therapy.

D. Psychosis (a loss of contact with reality)
   1. Work with another professional (local medical doctor, psychiatrist, or psychologist).
   2. Since the brain chemistry is usually altered in psychosis, medication is needed. Thus, the referral should be made to a psychiatrist.

III. Physical problems. Of course, physical problems will need to be referred to the local medical doctor or psychiatrist but since spiritual and psychological factors may also be present, the counselor may wish to work with the doctor. The minister or layman should be especially alerted to the following physical problems that are often confused with psychological or spiritual problems.

A. Hyperkinetic (hyperactive) child
B. High or low blood-sugar levels
C. Thyroid problems
D. Organic brain syndrome of old age
E. Biochemical depression.

The Decision-Making Process

A chapter on the principles of counseling and on treatment measures would not be complete without considering the decision-making process. Helping the counselee in the decision-making process is one of the key areas with which the counselor must deal. Individuals often ask how they can know if they are making the right decision. I believe the answer to this lies in examining three criteria. These are feelings, logic, and God's standard—the Bible. When I see individuals getting into trouble over faulty decisions, it is usually because they are making their decisions according to feelings first, logic second, and God's Word last. Though feelings are the most unstable and the most unreliable of standards, many individuals run their entire lives on this basis. I have often heard a husband or wife say that they are getting a divorce because they don't feel they love their mate anymore. When I hear this, I am reminded of the wise words of King Solomon when he stated that there was "a way that seemed right unto a man but the end thereof was the way of death" (*see* Proverbs 14:12). I have seen many individuals ruin their lives because they subjectively did what seemed in their feelings to be the thing to do.

More stable than feelings in making decisions is logic. This is simply considering the advantages and disadvantages of both sides of a decision and making the logical choice. Christians need to use this method more since many areas of decisions are not spoken of specifically in the Bible. We need to remember that God is the One who gives us our logic, and He wants us to use it. Of course, the danger with logic is that man is basically selfish, and without the guidance of the Holy Spirit, he will often choose a selfish course.

The best criterion for making decisions is God's Word. What is recorded in God's Word about a decision? Also related to God's Word is prayer, the conviction of the Holy Spirit, and advice from godly men.

10 Drugs Used in Psychiatry

Psychopharmacology in the Forefront

In the past, psychoanalysis has been the major thrust in
psychiatry, but today psychopharmacology is coming to the
forefront. Since many psychological problems have
biological components and since the Lord usually works
by natural means, I believe God is in agreement with the
major asset drugs have contributed to psychiatric therapy.
An adequate knowledge of psychotherapeutic drugs can be
of much practical importance to a Christian psychiatrist. In
accordance with the upsurge of drug usage in psychiatry,
the following discussion focuses on four problems often
seen in psychiatry or general practice.

Schizophrenia

The term *schizophrenia* was made famous by Eugen
Bleuler. In the early nineteen hundreds he described the
four A's that have come to be associated with schizophrenics. These are inappropriate affect, loose associations,
ambivalence, and autistic thinking. He also, as other authors previously, had described the secondary symptoms
such as hallucinations and delusions that may be present. I

167

too have observed all these symptoms in patients, and I am convinced the condition termed *schizophrenia* exists largely as described in classical terms. For instance, I have seen patients smile at circumstances that should have provoked a serious affect. I have listened to patients ramble from one topic to another with no discernible connection. I have observed the fear of patients responding to voices they heard incessantly. I have argued to no avail with individuals about their deeply ingrained delusions. These symptoms, consistent with a break with reality known as schizophrenia, are seen today as they were by Eugen Bleuler in the early nineteen hundreds.

Bleuler made practical suggestions for the treatment of schizophrenia that are still applicable today.[1] However, today a group of drugs known as the major tranquilizers have revamped the therapy in schizophrenia. Chlorpromazine and reserpine were introduced as tranquilizers in 1954, and these drugs resulted in an upsurge of interest in psychopharmacology. On these or other major tranquilizers most schizophrenics will improve. Of course, the amount of improvement varies with the individual. Recently a lady who presented to me was on the verge of a break with reality. She had not been sleeping, was having disturbing nightmares, and her speech indicated that distorted thinking was beginning. Because of major tranquilizers, this break was averted. Within a few weeks she was sleeping well with no nightmares, and the disturbance in cognition had cleared.

The drugs have a wide range of biochemical reactions in the body, and thus the specific reaction that accounts for the beneficial effects remains obscured. Even though the biochemical reactions are varied, these drugs have been proven safe and are not addicting.

Depression

Because depression has been so rampant in America, the introduction of antidepressive medication in 1954 has proven to be of immeasurable value. Seventy percent of a depressed population are helped by antidepressive medication. I personally have seen many patients respond with happier expressions, better moods, improved sleep, improved appetite, and increased ability to deal with their problems.

In depression there is often a biochemical defect. The antidepressive medication stimulates the limbic system of the brain which improves mood, sleep, and libido. These drugs inhibit the reticular activity system which also improves sleep. They also stimulate the hypothalamus which improves appetite. Finally, they increase neurohumoral deposits which are deficient in depressive disorders. These are biochemical problems—physical problems. Surely no one would argue with giving a diabetic insulin. Then why should anyone argue with replacing a natural neurohumoral deposit in depression?

Anxiety

In the past few decades a large number of minor tranquilizers have been developed to be given for anxiety. Unlike the major tranquilizers and antidepressants, these drugs produce physical tolerance and can be addicting. Thus, while the intrinsic qualities of these drugs have made them very popular, they are also potentially hazardous.

Hyperactive Children

Many children have suffered from secondary emotional problems that resulted because of their neurologically based hyperactivity, short attention span, and learning disability. Many of these emotional problems can now be prevented with the use of appropriate medication that slows the hyperactivity and increases the attention span. I have seen improvement in child after child—probably in greater than 90 percent of those treated.

Although the following chart is quite technical, I believe it will prove of benefit to those in professional fields. It summarizes several authors' writings on drugs used in psychiatry.[2-7]

Psychiatric Diagnosis: SCHIZOPHRENIA

Drugs	History of Drugs	*Approximate Dosages (in mg)/day		Side Effects

Drugs	History of Drugs	Drug	Out-Patient Dosage	In-Patient Dosage	Side Effects
Major Tranquilizers	1. Chlorpromazine and reserpine were introduced as tranquilizers in 1954.				1. Drowsiness
1. Phenothiazines					2. Parkinson
a. Aliphatic					Syndrome
Thorazine		1. Thorazine	30–400	400–1600	3. Allergic skin
b. Piperdine		2. Mellaril	50–400	75–800	reactions
Mellaril		3. Stelazine	4– 10	6– 30	4. Hematologic
c. Piperizine		4. Prolixin	1– 3	2– 20	disorders
Stelazine		5. Trilafon	8– 24	12– 65	5. Metabolic
Prolixin		6. Navane	6– 15	10– 60	effects (as
Trilafon		7. Haldol	2– 6	4– 15	menstrual
2. Thioxanthenes—					irregularities)
Navane					6. Restlessness
3. Butyrophenone					7. Jaundice
Haldol					
4. Molindone					
Moban					

---

*The dosages on this and following charts are not meant to be exact. Doctors needing details should refer to the *Physicians' Desk Reference.*

These charts are intended for academic use only. They are not intended to direct the use of any particular brand-named drug or treatment program.

Mode of Action of Major Tranquilizers

Phenothiazines are extremely active and have a wide range of biochemical reactions. Thus, it is difficult to know which reactions account for the desired effects. They affect parts of the brain as follows:

Cerebral cortex—not affected
Hypothalamus—inhibited
Reticular formation—inhibited
Limbic system—?
Thalamus—affects our neurotransmitters as dopamine
Neurohumoral deposits—inhibited

Other Comments on Major Tranquilizers

1. These agents decrease anxiety.
2. They have antiemetic, antipruritic, and analgesic effects.
3. They do not produce tolerance.
4. They have beneficial effects on cognitive disturbances and perceptual changes which are characteristic of schizophrenia.
5. When sedation is desired, thorazine is an appropriate drug. When as little sedation as possible is desired, stelazine is indicated.
6. In some conditions one major tranquilizer may be recommended over others. If depression is also present in schizophrenia, some therapists use mellaril. If agitation is prominent in schizophrenia, many therapists use haldol. For obsessive-compulsive neurosis, some therapists try haldol.
7. Phenothiazines may produce depression.
8. Phenothiazines are more effective than electric shock therapy or psychotherapy, in the treatment of schizophrenia.
9. Most patients improve. The amount of improvement varies.
10. The treatment of extrapyramidal side effects is with anticholinergics like artane (2 mg 3×/day).
11. Mellaril may delay ejaculation.
12. Most phenothiazines can be given by mouth or intramuscularly.

Psychiatric Diagnosis: DEPRESSION—1. Sad facial expression, 2. Problem with sleep, 3. Decreased appetite, 4. Feelings of hopelessness and helplessness, 5. Feelings of guilt, 6. Anxiety

Drugs	History of Drugs	*Approximate Dosages (in mg)/day	Side Effects

1. Tricyclic anti-depressants
  a. Imiprimine Tofranil, SK-Pramine
  b. Amitriptyline Elavil, Endep
  c. Doxepin Sinequan
  d. Nortriptyline Aventyl
  e. Desipramine Norpramine
2. Monoamine oxidase inhibitors (MAOI)
  a. Tranylcypramine Parnate
  b. Phenelzine Nardil
	1. The prototype of the tricyclics was tofranil. It was synthesized in 1954 and tested as a tranquilizer. It was accidentally found to have antidepressive activities.
	2. The first MAOI was Iproniazid. It was used in treating tuberculosis and accidentally found to have anti-depressive properties.
		1. The starting dose of tricyclics is often 25–50 mg three times/day.
		2. Tricyclics can be given all at bedtime. A typical dose is 150 mg at bedtime.
		3. A maximum dose is 250–300 mg per day.
			1. Tricyclics
			  a. Autonomic effects as dry mouth and difficulty in micturation
			  b. Cardiovascular effects as hypotension, tachycardia, and heart tracing changes
			  c. Endocrine effects as impotence, amenorrhea, decreased sex drive, and increased weight
			  d. Central nervous system effects as drowsiness, ataxia and tremor
			  e. Hematologic disorders
			2. MAOI
			  a. Similar to above
			  b. Hypertensive crisis

Mode of Action of Antidepressants

They stimulate the limbic system which improves mood.

They stimulate the hypothalamus which improves biologic functions such as sleep, appetite, and libido.

They inhibit the reticular activating system which improves sleep.

They increase neurohumoral deposists which are deficient in depressive disorders.

Other Comments on Antidepressants

1. Approximately 70% of a depressed population are helped by antidepressants.
2. They do not produce tolerance. They are not addicting.
3. It takes one to two weeks for antidepressants to take effect.
4. Tricyclics are as effective if given in a single dose at bedtime.
5. Therapy should usually be maintained for six months.
6. Tofranil and Elavil are probably used more than any other antidepressants.
7. If more sedation is desired to help a patient sleep better, Elavil is the drug of choice.
8. If the patient needs to be as alert as possible, Tofranil is the drug of choice.
9. Tofranil and Elavil are usually given by mouth but could be given intramuscularly.
10. Antidepressants should be used with caution in patients with increased intraocular pressure.
11. Tofranil will help in phobic reactions.
12. If a patient on MAOI should have a hypertensive crisis, he could be treated with Regitine (5 mg intravenously and repeated as needed).
13. Tofranil is the treatment of choice for bedwetting (enuresis).

Psychiatric Diagnosis: ANXIETY

Drugs	History of Drugs	*Approximate Dosages (in mg)/day	Side Effects
Minor Tranquilizers	A large number of	1. Valium 5–60 mg/day	Drowsiness
1. Benzodiazepines	minor tranquilizers	2. Librium 15–100 mg/day	Vertigo
a. Chlordiaz-	have been intro-	3. Vistaril 25–200 mg/day	Increased appetite
epoxide	duced in the last few	4. Miltown 800–2400	Headache
Librium	decades.	mg/day	Muscular weakness
b. Diazepam			Impaired judgment
Valium			Poor coordination
2. Propanediols			Hypotension
Meprobamate			Bizarre behavior
(Miltown)			Menstrual
3. Vistaril			irregularities

Mode of Action of Minor Tranquilizers

Their antianxiety effects are probably caused by their depressant influences on limbic structures.

They have a polysynaptic depressive effect that releases muscular spasms and thus muscular tension.

Other Comments on Minor Tranquilizers

1. They can produce tolerance.
2. They can be addicting.
3. They produce an immediate lift.
4. If minor tranquilizers are stopped abruptly, withdrawal symptoms may occur.
5. They should not be taken with alcohol.
6. Most minor tranquilizers can be given by mouth, intramuscularly or intravenously.

Psychiatric Diagnosis: MANIC-DEPRESSIVE PSYCHOSIS

Drugs	History of Drugs	*Approximate Dosages (in mg)/day	Side Effects
Lithium Carbonate	Cade first reported beneficial effects in the manic phase of manic depressive psychosis in 1949.	The starting dose of lithium carbonate is 300 mg–3×/day. A therapeutic level is a blood serum level of 1.0–1.5 mg/liter.	Drugged feeling Fine tremor Drowsiness Muscular twitch Slurred speech Nausea, vomiting Diarrhea Central nervous system effects

Other Comments on Lithium

1. Initially, serum levels should be monitored daily. Later they can be monitored every one to three months.
2. Mania breaks in five to ten days on lithium.
3. Contraindications to lithium therapy are brain and renal damage. Caution should be used if the patient has heart damage.

Psychiatric Diagnosis: HYPERKINETIC CHILDREN, SLEEPLESSNESS

Drugs	History of Drugs	*Approximate Dosages (in mg)/day	Side Effects
Ritalin		5–60 mg/day	
Dalmane		30 mg at bedtime	
Chloral hydrate		500 mg at bedtime	

Drugs and Referrals

Because the field of psychopharmacology is very broad, the Christian counselor must not expect every physician to be closely acquainted with the effects and side effects of each and every drug available. Most physicians have an adequate knowledge of all the drugs. However, when a fine point of decision arises, he should trust the judgment of those psychiatrists who have specialized in the field.

More than that, I count all things to be loss in view of the surpassing value of knowing Christ Jesus my Lord . . .

PHILIPPIANS 3:8 NAS

I said, Days should speak, and multitude of years should teach wisdom. But there is a spirit in man: and the inspiration of the Almighty giveth them understanding. Great men are not always wise: neither do the aged understand judgment.

JOB 32:7–9

11 The Counselor God Uses

A Letter From a Friend

My first year of medical school had ended. Soon I would face the decision of whether or not to specialize in psychiatry. This was the setting when one morning I received a letter from a friend. The following is an excerpt from that letter.

Probably the most effective prayer you could pray at this time is that God would break our independency, pride, and selfishness (*see* 2 Corinthians 4:16–18). God grant (Leviticus 26:19) that we would as His children have a profound change in our personalities after this summer together with Him! I hear myself say, "I believe this, I believe that. . . ." I'm not too impressed with my beliefs if His words do not constitute my life and make a profound change in my relationship with my wife, children, other Christians, and people in general. Beloved, God give us the realization that we do not really have anything on this earth but Christ. The closest person to us is no longer ourselves but Jesus Christ who is our very life!

I would later decide to go into psychiatry, and the principles laid down in that letter would further confirm in my mind the essential prerequisite for a Christian counselor.

According to King Solomon, who penned Proverbs, Song of Solomon and Ecclesiastes, a good counselor was a man who had wisdom and common sense. Solomon made reference to at least five characteristics that pertain to a wise man and thus, certainly to one who hopes to help others find wisdom. These characteristics are: He is in pursuit of God *(see* Proverbs 9:10); he knows God's Word in a living way *(see* Proverbs 16:20, 22–23); he knows the importance of prayer *(see* Proverbs 15:8); he values fellowship with godly people *(see* Proverbs 13:20); and he shares the Word of God *(see* Ecclesiastes 11:6).

In Pursuit of God

First, a wise man is one who hungers to know Christ more. As I reflect back on individuals I have known in the Christian life, and as I study the Word of God, one theme resounds as the characteristic far above all others. That is the profound truth expressed by Apostle Paul when he wrote, "More than that, I count all things to be loss in view of the surpassing value of knowing Christ Jesus my Lord ..." (Philippians 3:8 NAS). Paul was a man who utterly groaned to be more with Christ, to enjoy the sheer pleasure of His presence *(see* Philippians 1:21–24). Not only did Paul have this intense desire, but the same desire is found expressed over and over in the Old Testament, the New Testament, and by mighty men of God in more recent generations.

The Levites of the Old Testament days were priests chosen by the Lord for the specific purpose of ministering to Him. This reveals a very significant glimpse into the character of God and into what was in His heart—men who would be occupied much alone with Him. The New Testament continued with the same theme, and stated that we are priests chosen by God for the same purpose of showing His praise, thereby being impressed with Christ alone.

There is no greater calling than to be occupied with Christ our Lord—not with what we are doing *for* Him, but *with* Him.

King David, probably one of the best known kings of all ages, is another example of an individual whose one desire in life was to know God intimately and behold His beauty (*see* Psalms 27:4). David said this was not one of many desires but his one desire. Thus, it is worth noting that the Lord said of David that he was a man after His heart. God used David to change the kingdom because of this trait and not because of David's abilities.

Apostle John recorded that God is actually seeking a particular type of man. The man God is seeking is the one who will be absorbed in really worshipping Him. Apostle John in John 4:23–24 recorded that God seeks true worshippers who will worship Him in spirit and reality.

Edward M. Bounds, in his classic book *Power Through Prayer* points out that the men who have accomplished the most for Christ were men who spent much time alone with Him. John Wesley spent two hours daily in prayer. Martin Luther spent at least two hours daily with the Lord. John Welch, a famous Scottish evangelist, spent eight hours a day with the Lord. I personally have known a few individuals who were deeply impressed with Christ. Of the counselors I have known, they have had the most insight. The lesson for us is perhaps best expressed by the modern-day author Aiden Tozer—Be in "pursuit of God."

The Bible is filled with the stories of such men. For example, Enoch was in pursuit of God. In Genesis 5:24 is recorded the following: "And Enoch walked with God: and he was not; for God took him." Also, Moses was in pursuit of God. In Exodus 33:11 is recorded that "And the Lord spake unto Moses face to face, as a man speaketh unto his friend." God looks for such men. In 2 Chronicles 16:9 is recorded, "For the eyes of the Lord run to and fro throughout the whole earth, to shew himself strong in the behalf of them whose heart is perfect toward him. . . ." The same is true today—*God is looking throughout the whole earth today for men in pursuit of Him.*

A Supernatural Power

A second characteristic of the man of wisdom is that he knows God's Word in a living way *(see* Proverbs 16: 22–23). This thought was expressed by Jeremiah when he stated, ". . . thy Word was unto me the joy and rejoicing of mine heart . . ." (Jeremiah 15:16). Apostle Paul expressed the same ideal when he stated, "And now, brethren, I commend you to God, and to the word of His grace, which is able to build you up . . ." (Acts 20:32). The Lord Jesus Christ further expressed the importance of the thought when He stated, ". . . the words that I speak unto you, they are spirit, and they are life" (John 6:63). In recent times, God has used Watchman Nee to express this concept that His Word is more than a documentary to be studied, but is ". . . quick, and powerful, and sharper than any twoedged sword . . ." (Hebrews 4:12).

The Word of God not only instructs us, corrects us, and reproves us, but perhaps most of all, nourishes us. This is a concept that for years has seemingly remained subdued. At least this appears to be true in general and certainly was in my life. I never shall forget when I began to take the Scriptures as more than instructions and corrections but also nourishment and enjoyment. Through memorizing specific verses that met my needs, through praying God's Word back to Him, and through enjoying it with others, the Scriptures came alive to me.

God's words to us as recorded in the Bible by godly men, not only provide us with spiritual nourishment but also protection in our age of spiritual and mental confusion. This age of confusion is one in which men base their eternal destinies on what others believe, while others believe many and varied things. What really matters is not what others believe, but what God's Word says! In psychiatry, I have been exposed to concepts that just are not scriptural.

Other concepts are helpful and do not disagree with Scripture. I have found the best way to evaluate the concepts I am exposed to is by comparing them to the Word of God which I have memorized. Not only has God's Word helped in evaluating concepts of psychiatry, but also the many and varied Christian views. A Christian without the Word of God memorized is open prey to the enemy and confusion of our day.

For me, the most valuable aspect of God's Word in regard to evaluation, however, has not been with respect to others. Rather, it has been the equally valuable source to evaluate whether thoughts and conflicts within myself have been merely of myself or of God. In Hebrews 4:12 Apostle Paul recorded, "For the word of God is quick, and powerful, and sharper than any twoedged sword, piercing even to the dividing asunder of soul and spirit, and of the joints and marrow, and is a discerner of the thoughts and intents of the heart." Thus, the Word of God helps us distinguish between "soulish" issues (those coming merely from ourselves) and spiritual issues.

In conclusion, since there are so many books on counseling and psychology to which we may turn for help, we might do well to remind ourselves as did King Solomon when he stated, "The words of the wise are as goads, and as nails fastened by the masters of assemblies, which are given from one shepherd. And further, by these, my son, be admonished: of making many books there is no end; and much study is a weariness of the flesh" (Ecclesiastes 12:11-12). By analogy, we will do well to remind ourselves of the importance of God's Word over even many books of psychiatry and psychology, though these can be helpful.

When considering the effect of God's Word upon our lives, I believe one more point is of utmost importance. I would like to support this point both scientifically and biblically. First, scientific data has shown the importance of the unconscious mind. A neurosurgeon named Wilder Graves Penfield found out that by touching electrodes to

different areas of the brain, individuals were able to remember specific past events and the feeling that went
along with the event.[1] It was found that current-day events
often trigger feelings of the past without the event itself
being recalled. Thus, an individual may hear a song and
feel sad but not know why he feels sad until later, when he
remembers how the song related to a past event.

Feelings of rejection often relate more to past events
than to the current-day situation. For example, a man
feared being rejected by others. Few current-day events
could explain those feelings, but in therapy, it was discovered he feared rejection by others when he was young.
Now, the least event could trigger these feelings. It was as
though a tape of these feelings of the past were being replayed. Of course, not only may the feelings of the past be
replayed, but the actual event may be remembered also.
Also, the event may be recalled without the event. Thus,
three possibilities exist.

In any event, all of this simply says that the unconscious
mind is an important factor in conscious behavior, and significant events that have been recorded by the brain do
affect present behavior. I believe this speaks to the tremendous importance of saturating our minds with the
Word of God. As the Word of God is enjoyed and
memorized, it sinks into the subconscious and is there for
years to come. It can be a significant determinant of behavior. David expressed it this way:

> Wherewithal shall a young man cleanse his way? by taking
> heed thereto according to thy word.
>
> Thy word have I hid in mine heart, that I might not sin
> against thee.
>
> PSALMS 119:9, 11

All of the above points to the fact that the Word of God
can be of immeasurable power in our lives. Recently I was
meditating on Hebrews 11:3: "Through faith we under-

stand that the worlds were framed by the word of God, so
that things which are seen were not made of things which
do appear." The words contained in that verse encouraged
me to do research on the power of God's Word. I found that
if one traveled at the speed of light (186,000 miles per
second) he would be 100,000 years old if he traveled
across the diameter of the Milky Way.[2] Furthermore,
there are several hundred billion galaxies like the Milky
Way. My mind could hardly comprehend the size of the
universe. And then I thought, *If God created the universe
by His word, then what could His word do in my life?*

Prayer and Counseling Success

Much can be said of the importance of God's Word, but
prayer makes the realities of God's Word personal to us and
enables us to share that application with those we seek to
counsel. Thus, a third characteristic of a godly man is that
he knows the importance of prayer. For through prayer we
gain insight, and through prayer the insights we share with
others are made significant to them. The danger in Christian counseling is a reliance upon methods rather than
God's power made possible through prayer. God uses
methods, and much can be learned didactically that aids in
counseling. However, our methods are always secondary
in importance to God's power. Accordingly, James recorded that Elias was a godly man but was ". . . subject to
like passions as we are, and he prayed earnestly . . ."
(James 5:17). To be sure, more can be accomplished by
prayer than we ever dream possible.

Prayer is communion with God. This communion is possible because of Christ's death for us and because of His
indwelling Holy Spirit. The only prayer possible for the
non-Christian is one that expresses a personal belief and
reliance upon Christ as Savior. I recently heard a lady who
was not a Christian say that she prayed about a problem
and subsequently felt better. I do not doubt that talking it

over helped her feelings, but God will not answer such prayer. Prayer is only possible through a relationship with God through Christ. Once that relationship has been established by placing faith in Christ, God longs for us to talk with Him. In Proverbs, Solomon recorded that God delights in our prayers (*see* Proverbs 15:8).

Prayer may consist of praise (*see* Psalms 9:11), confession (*see* 1 John 1:9), or thanksgiving and supplication (*see* Philippians 4:6).[3] Confession relieves us of our sense of guilt. Being thankful is an encouragement to both us and our gracious Father, and supplication can accomplish unlimited means, since it gives God the opportunity to either answer our primary request or the desire in the request. But the prayer that I have found the most helpful of those above is praise. In praise I become absorbed in someone other than myself. Many problems are a result of self-involvement. Praise can remedy this. Moses became so discouraged when he was self-involved with his eyes on self rather than God, that he wanted to die. His prayers indicated self-concern more than God-concern. Christ also pointed to priority when He stated, "But seek ye first the Kingdom of God" (*see* Matthew 6:33). This applies to our prayers as well, lest our very prayers become self-centered. I have found singing songs to the Lord or praying His words of praise back to Him of utmost *practical* importance for mental as well as spiritual health.

I have found several helpful "how to's" concerning prayer, the most important of which is just to exercise ourselves to do it. Then God will gradually teach us important applications and wonders of prayer. It is recorded in the Bible that Moses talked with God as a friend to a friend. This kind of deep prayer relationship developed primarily because Moses simply talked much with God. I am sure that initially Moses did not know all of the various aspects of prayer, but he knew God as his friend as well as his God and felt free to talk with Him. God longs for us to consider Him a friend, and to talk with Him and call upon Him during moments throughout the day. I believe this is the most important "how to."

A Secret to Wisdom

A fourth characteristic of a wise man who hopes to counsel others is that he knows the importance of fellowship with godly men. In Proverbs 13:20 Solomon recorded, "He that walketh with wise men shall be wise ..." and in Proverbs 27:17 Solomon recorded, "Iron sharpeneth iron; so a man sharpeneth the countenance of his friend." The wise King Solomon continued with the same theme in Ecclesiastes when he wrote, "Two are better than one; because they have a good reward for their labour. For if they fall, the one will lift up his fellow; but woe to him that is alone when he falleth; for he hath not another to help him up" (Ecclesiastes 4:9–10). It is interesting to note that together the condition of falling is only a possibility but alone is a certainty.

Fellowship with godly men has taught me much about counseling both from a didactic view as well as practical experience. From other men, I have learned techniques: I have learned to listen, I have learned the importance of keeping confident what others tell me, but most of all, I have been exposed to the measure of the grace of Christ in their lives.

Witnessing for Christ

Finally, the wise counselor is one who sows the Word of God. He is one who testifies of Christ to others both by his actions and his words. God promises to bless His Words (*see* Isaiah 55:11), and not our words. Whether an individual allows this Word to prosper for him is much of his responsibility, but our job is to share it in an appropriate manner. By analogy, if not by direct implication, we can learn a lesson from King Solomon who wrote, "In the morning sow thy seed, and in the evening withhold not thine hand: for thou knowest not whether shall prosper, either this or that, or whether they both shall be alike good" (Ecclesiastes 11:6).

Qualities of a Christian Counselor

In addition to basic characteristics that are needed by all Christians and thus by a godly counselor, there are also qualities that are uniquely vital for a Christian counselor. To a degree these qualities can be learned, but more significantly, they are gifts from the Lord. I have chosen to discuss ten of these qualities that have become significant to me.

Have an Attitude of Acceptance

One quality that a counselee is seeking in a counselor is an attitude of acceptance. Problems are normal, and no one is above them. I have heard others imply that their fellow Christians should not have problems, but little do they realize that this is one of the major means God uses to conform us to His image. Ministers and deacons have problems just as everyone else, but they may feel ashamed to share their problems or may feel that no one would accept that they, too, need understanding and counsel. We all have problems, and God desires that we accept and counsel one another. I first began to grow rapidly in the Christian life when I found a couple of other brothers who accepted me with no conditions.

Be a Good Listener

A second quality of a godly counselor is that he is a good listener. He listens with interest, and without fidgeting or hurrying. He listens without interruptions and shows warmth through the expression of his eyes. Further, a good listener allows the person to finish sharing what he perceives his problem to be before helping him gain insight. He uses properly inserted questions which initially are used to obtain information and clarify issues, but can later be used to provoke thinking and help the counselee reach his own conclusions. Elihu, a counselor in Old Testament times, knew the importance of listening when he stated, "Behold, I waited for your words, I listened to your reasonings, While you pondered what to say. I even paid close attention to you . . ." (*see* Job 32:11–12 NAS). Many are willing to speak, but few are willing to listen.

Be Suggestive and Confronting

A third quality of a godly counselor is that he knows how to be suggestive. There is a time for suggestive statements, and often these will be received when a statement would be rejected. I have found suggestive phrases helpful. However, a good counselor also knows when to be direct and confronting. In Proverbs 27:6 is recorded the following, "Faithful are the wounds of a friend. . . ."

In summary, there are times to be suggestive, and times to be confronting. The good counselor can discern which to use.

Interject Scripture

A fourth quality of the godly counselor is that he knows how and when to interject Scripture. Proper timing and readiness are important. Once the counselee knows the counselor really cares, Scripture can usually be shared without any offense. The Scripture must meet the specific need of the individual, and a few verses are preferable to many. Likewise, I have found it helpful to copy the verses down for the counselee. At the appropriate time, prayer with a counselee is also of great benefit.

Use Proper Attitude

A fifth quality that is helpful is the particular attitude the counselor employs to help various personalities. Various attitudes are: matter-of-factness, firm kindness, active friendliness, and passive friendliness. Christ was often matter-of-fact, and yet he knew when to use firm kindness or another attitude. A counselor might use a matter-of-fact attitude with a brother living in sin, firm kindness with a depressed brother, active friendliness with those who really want and need encouragement, and passive friendliness with those who have paranoid trends. Each person is different, and by being sensitive to his spirit, the counselor can employ an attitude to which the counselee can best respond.

Have an Unwavering Purpose for Christ

A sixth quality of a Christian counselor is an unwavering purpose for Christ. There are thousands of individuals today who are looking for someone with a purpose for living—someone who knows where he is heading—someone who is living for Christ.

Be Personal

Counselees need counselors who are warm, open, honest, genuine, and very personal. To be open and honest themselves, they must sense the same from the counselor. They want to sense that the counselor is personally interested in them and their problems. As has been pointed out by William Glasser, most who need psychiatric help have not been able to fulfill two basic needs in life—love and self-worth.[4] A warm, personal counselor can be at least one person who can give them love and self-worth. The Scriptures repeatedly point to the need to be personal (*see* Galatians 4:19, Proverbs 12:25, Philippians 1:3–8).

Be Unshockable

A young man in my office recently commented, "I could never have shared these things with Reverend Q." He went on to indicate how shocked his minister would have been. A good counselor does not act shocked upon hearing a counselee's story. This only frightens the counselee and prevents him from sharing the guilt he may so need to share, and prevents him from learning how to deal with it effectively. Christ was not shocked with the problems of men for ". . . he knew what was in man" (John 2:25). When Christ was helping the woman of Sychar (*see* John 4), he did not seem shocked at her past. He dealt with it straightforwardly and effectively.

Be Confident

A good counselor offers the counselee realistic hope. He is confident in Christ, in his ability as a counselor through Christ, and in what Christ can accomplish in the counselee. If I think I can help a person, I let him know it. If I think a depressed person will start feeling better, I tell him so. I try to offer what I consider to be realistic hope. I do try to be realistic. For example, I would not tell a person with an I.Q. of 80 that I felt he could go to college. Rather, I would help him make realistic plans. In Hebrews 10:35–36 is recorded, "Cast not away therefore your confidence, which hath great recompense of reward. For ye have need of patience, that, after ye have done the will of God, ye might receive the promise."

Have a Sense of Humor

A counselor needs a sense of humor. He deals with many serious problems daily and without a sense of humor, the load can be too much. He needs at times to be able to help his counselee have this same sense of humor. For example, I have found that obsessive-compulsive people often begin to improve when they can start to laugh at their perfectionism.

> Much can be learned from godly
> counselors of the past. Although not
> applying directly to Christian coun-
> selors, Paul said, ". . . join in follow-
> ing my example. . . ."
>
> PHILIPPIANS 3:17 NAS

12 Four Biblical Counselors

One of the best methods of learning how to counsel effectively is to study men of the past who were skilled in this
field. Two counselors from Old Testament days and two
from New Testament days offer significant information in
the field of counseling. Solomon and Elihu come to us from
the Old Testament. Christ and the Apostle Paul are examples from the New Testament.

Elihu

The record of Elihu's counseling occupies six chapters
in the Book of Job, thus Elihu is one of the earliest godly
counselors recorded by God. Although Elihu is not well
known, he demonstrated much in the way of wise counsel,
and a little in the way of poor counsel. Thanks to Elihu, we
can learn much from his mistakes.

Job was a friend of Elihu's. Job was a godly man, but
Satan argued that Job was godly because of the benefits he
had received. Satan was granted permission from God to
try Job with suffering. Job began to suffer much physically
and mentally. He lost his health, his wealth, and his family.
Four friends of Job's came to counsel with him concerning

his condition. Initially all four did well. They just listened, and Job must have greatly benefited from their company. Then the first three counselors made their mistakes.

The first three counselors were Eliphaz, Bildad, and Zophar. These counselors made four significant errors. First, they proved to be talkers and not listeners. They had much true and eloquent advice, but the advice was not practical. They were too directive, too fast. They were legalistic and dogmatic. Secondly, they failed to convey an attitude of paramount importance. They were not understanding but rather, harsh and cruel. They were accusers, not counselors. Thirdly, their discourses are filled with evidences of pride, and pride is downfall to any counselor. Finally, they had an inadequate concept of God. They saw God as being petty in His relations with man and failed to see the glory, grace, and mercy of God. These four errors accounted for their failure as counselors and will account for failure among counselors today.

Elihu was different from the other counselors. He was much younger. He was a better listener. He was polite, sincere, and honest. He indicated depth in his thinking. He had a higher concept of God. He knew the importance of expressing himself, but at the appropriate time. Some quotes from and about Elihu are:

> Now Elihu had waited to speak to Job because they were years older than he (Job 32:4 NAS).

> I said, Days should speak, and multitude of years should teach wisdom. But there is a spirit in man: and the inspiration of the Almighty giveth them understanding. Great men are not always wise: neither do the aged understand judgment (Job 32:7–9).

> Lo, all these things worketh God oftentimes with man, To bring back his soul from the pit, to be enlightened with the light of the living (Job 33:29–30).

> I will fetch my knowledge from afar, and will ascribe righteousness to my Maker (Job 36:3).

Although Elihu also committed errors, God did not rebuke him as He did the other three counselors when He stated, ". . . My wrath is kindled against thee, and against thy two friends: for ye have not spoken of me the thing that is right . . ." (Job 42:7). Incidentally, God was merciful to the three counselors even though they were wrong, and He accepted Job's prayer in their behalf.

Additional comments on the counseling of Elihu have been made by Scofield.[1]

Solomon

Of all the men mentioned in the Bible with the exception of Christ, Solomon outranks them all as a counselor. Solomon is a counselor's counselor. His therapeutic approach is directive. His counseling approach could be very directive because his counsel agreed with the counsel of God. In fact, God gave Solomon's writings on counseling more merit than any other. They were, in fact, God's thoughts on counseling. Nowhere else in the Bible is such length and detail on counseling permitted as in Proverbs. The Book of Proverbs contains the secrets to a wealth of wisdom. In this book, Solomon covered such topics as rules for mental health, descriptions of sociopaths, descriptions of the sensuous woman, the road to wisdom, characteristics of the wise, and rules for raising children. Solomon dealt very specifically with these and other issues, and I have been impressed with the similarity between his descriptions of certain conditions and that described in psychiatric texts.

The Book of Proverbs may be compared with two other books also written by Solomon—Song of Solomon and Ecclesiastes. In Ecclesiastes Solomon described his search for meaning in life. He tried wealth, sex, humanitarian efforts, and intellectual pursuit. His conclusion was "Vanity of vanities . . ." (Ecclesiastes 1:2). In Song of Solomon, Solomon wrote a love story. If one abstracts somewhat, he may consider this an analogy of the love Christ has for each one of His children and the resulting fulfillment that one finds in Christ alone. Watchman Nee in his book *Song of Songs* has so aptly contrasted the "vanity of vanities" conclusion in Ecclesiastes with the "song of songs" conclusion in the Song of Solomon (*see* Song of Solomon 1:1). Thus, in Song of Solomon, God has revealed the beginning of wisdom. The beginning of wisdom is to be in pursuit of a deep relationship with Jesus Christ. In Proverbs the expanse of that wisdom is broadened into much practical advice.

Jesus Christ

Although Solomon was the wisest man who ever lived, he was not the wisest counselor. That distinction belongs to One who was not only man but also God—Jesus Christ. Jesus Christ was the Counselor of counselors. There are six areas in which He excelled in counseling.

The Lord Jesus Christ had perfect insight into a man's problem. Insight is of paramount importance in helping others in counseling. The therapist must have insight into what the real problems are, and he must be able to help the patient gain this insight. Christ could do both of these.

As stated previously, Christ was an expert at asking questions. He used questions to teach, to help others gain insight, and to rebuke irresponsible behavior. The ability to use questions in a counseling situation is an art of invaluable measure.

Thirdly, Christ really cared for those He counseled. This is something people can just sense. It is something innate that we can usually read in others. Really caring for a person accounts for much of his improvement. Most people with emotional problems have had difficulty finding others they can relate to and who give them a feeling of self-worth. Christ knew how to be matter-of-fact, rebuking, or friendly; and yet, He could relate that He really cared.

Fourthly, Christ could counsel others because of His close relationship with God the Father. This is a prerequisite to doing Christian counseling. Someone who walks and talks with God knows himself, his weaknesses, and his strengths through God. He understands man and has insight into problems. He has available to him the wisdom of God. How can one help others learn how to live if he does not know himself through his relationship with God? Christ knew the Word of God. In fact, He *was* the Word of God. The Word of God and the relationship with God developed through the Word, and prayer forms the foundation of Christian counseling.

Christ understood a man's problems. He knew what the man needed to do to change and deal with his problems. And, finally, He knew how to motivate the man to change. Christ could help an individual formulate a plan of action to deal with his problems.

The sixth reason Christ excelled in counseling was His balance. He knew when to be overtly directive and when to ask questions to help the person gain insight. He knew when something that happened to an individual in the past needed to be dealt with, and when to deal with the here and now. Christ knew the importance of feelings, and how to focus on needed behavioral changes. In both Christianity and psychiatry there is often a trend toward extremes; Christ had perfect balance.

Apostle Paul

There is yet one individual who should be mentioned as an example for Christian counselors because it was he and not Sigmund Freud who first wrote concerning the psychic forces that play on the mind of man. Apostle Paul, in writing to early Christians, explained that their minds would be drawn between an old nature and a new nature; that they could choose what to do in each case. The analogies are not exact, but similar. The *id* would correspond to the old nature. The *superego* would correspond to the new nature (indwelling Christ), or the conscience of a non-Christian. The *ego* would correspond to the will. However, Paul goes even deeper into the makeup of man and talks about a body, a soul (consisting of a mind, emotion, and will), a spirit, the flesh, a good but weak law of the mind, an evil law of the members, a supreme law of the Spirit, an external deadening law, and how all of these parts interrelate (*see* Romans 6, 7, 8; Hebrews 4:12; 1 Thessalonians 5:23; and 1 Corinthians 4:16). There are indeed, some similarities between the writings of Sigmund Freud and the teachings of Saint Paul, but there is no doubt, that Saint Paul was the greater analyst of the two.

Ministers face a difficult problem in deciding if, when, and how to refer to a professional.

THE AUTHOR

13   Professional Help—When and How to Refer

Is this a spiritual problem or a mental problem? Should I refer this counselee to a psychiatrist? Will the psychiatrist take away the client's faith in God?

The above are typical questions that ministers have. They are valid questions. Below are given some guidelines on when to refer to another professional.

If the client is suicidal or homicidal, then the minister should refer. The counselee may need immediate hospitalization to prevent him from harming himself or others. Such statements as, "Life doesn't seem worth living"; "I wish I were dead"; and, "Everything seems hopeless," indicate suicidal thoughts and plans. The counselee should be asked if he has had suicidal thoughts, plans, or attempts. If he has, he should be referred. Likewise, the counselee should be asked about any desires to harm others. If he has any, then again, he should be referred.

If a person has lost contact with reality, then he should be referred. He may have delusions (as a fear that the Mafia is after him), or he may be having hallucinations (seeing or hearing things not present). These individuals often misinterpret whatever is said to them, and thus, counseling alone is usually not effective. With medication, plus coun-

195

seling, a chronic mental case can be prevented, and the counselee can be restored to reality.

If a counselee is extremely euphoric, has pressure of speech, and is extremely hyperactive, he may be manic. There seems to be a genetic and chemical abnormality here, and dramatic results can be obtained with a drug known as lithium. With the drug, most counselees return to normal. Without the drug, the counselee is dangerous to himself, makes extremely poor judgments which can result in financial failure, and is impossible to counsel. Such a patient needs referral to a professional.

Another problem with an organic base which needs referral is the hyperkinetic reaction of childhood. Many very hyperactive children fall into this category. They respond well with drugs. With appropriate medication, their activity level is normal, they can sit still when necessary, and secondary emotional problems are prevented from developing.

Of course, individuals with mental retardation or organic brain syndrome should be referred. An individual with an incapacitating neurosis (can't sleep or function socially and biologically) may need referral. Individuals with apparent physical problems (instant blindness or paralysis) should be referred.

Perhaps the question of when to refer could be simplified by listing four classifications which seem to summarize many of the cases which need referral. They are:

1. Refer anyone suicidal. Remember that many people who are extremely depressed are also suicidal.

2. Refer anyone homicidal.

3. Refer anyone when the minister realizes that the problem is beyond his ability and/or he feels uncomfortable trying to handle it.

4. Refer anyone when the minister cannot handle the case adequately because of a lack of time in his schedule.

The above list is not comprehensive but does indicate

the type of problems that need to be referred. Of course, the basic question in considering referral is whether the problem is spiritual, mental, or physical. I personally believe this line is hard to draw at times. For example, under stress many Christians choose not (or just do not know *how*) to turn to the Lord for help. Thus, the stress increases and mental symptoms develop. Is this a spiritual or mental problem? Certainly, both are involved.

Referrals may be from a minister to a psychiatrist, a psychologist, or an individual in another field. A referral may be from any one of the above to any other of the above. This was discussed in chapter 1. However, I feel that it would be helpful to mention one other point. I have found that when treating a counselee referred by a minister, a brief phone call periodically to keep each other informed can be of much help to the counselee.

Christian Psychiatry—Does it Exist?

Christian psychiatry—does it exist? I believe it does, and I have attempted in this book to present an integration of sound theology with valid psychiatric knowledge into concepts known simply as Christian Psychiatry. I have enjoyed writing the book and hope the reader has benefited from it.

Source Notes

Chapter 1

1. Newsletter from Audio-Digest Foundation, California, July 1973.
2. Ibid.
3. Robert Shannon, Lecture on Psychodynamics, University of Arkansas Medical Center, 1972.
4. Solomon and Patch, *Handbook*.
5. Calvin S. Hall and Gardner Lindzey, *Theories of Personality* (New York: John Wiley and Sons, Inc., 1957).
6. Ibid.
7. Ibid.
8. Ibid.
9. Gary Collins, "The Pulpit and the Couch," *Christianity Today* 19 (August 1975): 5-9.
10. Hall, *Theories*.
11. A. M. Nicoli, "A New Dimension of the Youth Culture," *American Journal of Psychiatry* 131 (1974): 396-401.
12. W. P. Wilson, "Mental Health Benefits of Religious Salvation," *Diseases of the Nervous System* 33 (1972): 382-386.
13. C. Christensen, "Religious Conversion," *Archives of General Psychiatry* 9 (1963): 207-216.
14. E. M. Pattison, "Social and Psychological Aspects of Religion in Psychotherapy," *Journal of Nervous and Mental Diseases*

141 (1965): 586-597.

15. S. Janus and B. Bess, "Drug Abuse, Sexual Attitudes, Political Radicalization, and Religious Practices of College Seniors and Public School Teachers," *American Journal of Psychotherapy* 130 (1973): 187-191.

16. L. Allison, "Adaptive Regression and Intense Religious Experiences," *Journal of Nervous and Mental Diseases* 145 (1967): 452-463.

17. S. Freud, "The Future of an Illusion" (1927), in *Complete Psychological Works*, standard ed. 21, trans. J. Strachey (London: Hobarth Press, 1961), 5-56.

18. S. Freud, "Obsessive Actions and Religious Practice" (1907), Ibid. 9: 117-127.

19. S. Freud, "Totem and Taboo" (1912), Ibid 13: 1-161.

20. W. P. Wilson, "The Religious Life of Patients with Affective Disorders," *Diseases of the Nervous System* 30 (1969): 438-486.

21. B. G. Meyerson and L. Staller, "A Psychoanalytical Interpretation of the Crucifixion," *Psychoanalysis* 49 (4) 1962: 117-118.

22. P. Bergman, "A Religious Conversion in the Course of Psychotherapy," *American Journal of Psychotherapy* 7 (1953): 41-58.

23. A. Bronner, "Psychotherapy with Religious Patients," *American Journal of Psychotherapy* 18 (1964): 475-487.

24. C. G. Jung, *Mysterium Coniunctionis* 14, trans. R. Hull (New York: Bollingen Foundation, Inc., 1963).

25. E. Fromm, *Escape from Freedom* (New York and Boston: Rinehart and Co., Inc., 1941).

26. A. Adler, *The Individual Psychology of Alfred Adler*, ed. and annotated by Ansbacher and Ansbacher (New York: Basic Books, Inc., 1956): 460-464.

27. W. James, *The Varieties of Religious Experience* (New York: Collier Books, 1961).

28. S. Freud, "Obsessive Actions and Religious Practice."

29. C. G. Jung, *Mysterium Coniunctionis*.

30. W. James, *Varieties*.

31. A. Adler, *The Individual Psychology*.

32. E. Fromm, *Escape From Freedom*.

33. C. Christensen, "Religious Conversion."

34. L. Allison, "Adaptive Regression."

35. E. M. Pattison, "Social and Psychological Aspects of Religion in Psychotherapy."

36. A. Bronner, "Psychotherapy with Religious Patients."

37. P. Bergman, "A Religious Conversion."

38. B. G. Meyerson and L. Staller, "A Psychoanalytical Interpretation of the Crucifixion."

39. W. P. Wilson, "Mental Health Benefits of Religious Salvation," *Diseases of the Nervous System* 33 (1972): 382-386.

40. W. P. Wilson, "The Religious Life of Patients with Affective Disorders."

41. A. M. Nicoli, "A New Dimension."

42. Gary Collins, "The Pulpit and the Couch."

43. Ibid.

44. Ibid.

45. Howard Hendricks, "Counseling," Lecture at Dallas Theological Seminary, Dallas, Texas, 1970.

46. Doug Wilson, "A Fresh Perspective on Biblical Counseling," unpublished, December 1975.

47. W. E. Vine, *Expository Dictionary of New Testament Words* (New Jersey: Fleming H. Revell Co., 1966).

Chapter 2

1. Paul Tournier, *Guilt and Grace* (New York: Harper and Row 1962).

2. W. E. Vine, *Expository Dictionary.*

3. *The American College Dictionary*, 1963, s.v. "debt," "works," "law."

4. Lewis Sperry Chafer, *Grace* (Michigan: Zondervan Publishing House, 1922).

5. Lewis S. Chafer, *Salvation* (Michigan: Zondervan Publishing House, 1917).

6. Lewis S. Chafer, *True Evangelism* (Michigan: Zondervan Publishing House, 1967).

7. Harry Ironside, *Full Assurance* (Chicago: Moody Press, 1937).

8. Watchman Nee, *Sit, Walk, Stand* (Pennsylvania: Christian Literature Crusade, 1957).

9. C. I. Scofield, Scofield Notes on Galatians, *Scofield Reference Bible* (New York: Oxford University Press, 1945).

10. Charles Haddon Spurgeon, *Spurgeon Sermon Notes* (Michigan: Zondervan Publishing House, 1857).

11. Paul Tournier, *Guilt and Grace* (New York: Harper and Row, 1962).

Chapter 3

1. Lewis S. Chafer, *Systematic Theology* II (Texas: Dallas Seminary Press, 1947).

2. Bill Gothard, Basic Youth Conflicts Seminar (Kansas City, November 1972).

3. Charles Hodge, *Systematic Theology* II (New York: Charles Scribner's Sons, 1871).

4. Witness Lee, "Spirit, Soul, and Body," *The Stream* 4:1 (1966).

5. Don Meredith et al., Christian Family Life Seminar (Dallas, Texas, June, 1973).

6. Watchman Nee, *The Spiritual Man* 1 (New York: Christian Fellowship Publishers, Inc., 1968).

7. Augustus H. Strong, *Systematic Theology* (New York: A. C. Armstrong and Son, 1886).

8. W. E. Vine, *Expository Dictionary*.

9. Leonard L. Heston, "The Genetics of Schizophrenia."

Chapter 4

1. Thomas P. Detre and Henry G. Jarecki, *Modern Psychiatric Treatment* (Philadelphia: J. B. Lippincott Co., 1971).

2. Merril Eaton and Margaret Peterson, *Psychiatry*.

3. Robert F. Shannon and Joe T. Backus, "Treatment of Depression," *Journal of Arkansas Medical Society*, January 1974.

4. *Diagnostic and Statistical Manual of Mental Disorders*, 2nd ed. (Washington, D.C.: American Psychiatric Association, 1968).

5. Harold I. Kaplan and Alfred M. Freedman, *Comprehensive Textbook of Psychiatry* (Baltimore: Williams and Wilkins Company, 1967).

6. Ibid.

7. E. M. Berman and H. I. Lief, "Marital Therapy from a Psychiatric Perspective: An Overview," *American Journal of Psychiatry* 132, no. 6 (June 1975), 583-592.

8. Beulah C. Bosselman, *Neurosis and Psychosis,* 3rd ed. (Illinois: C. C. Thomas, 1969).

9. J. R. Smythies et al., *Biological Psychiatry: A Review of Ancient Advances* (New York: Springer-Verlag, Inc., 1968).

Chapter 5

1. Manual for the Psychiatry Department of the University of the Arkansas Medical Center, Little Rock, Arkansas, 1972.

Chapter 6

1. Marcus A. Krupp and Milton J. Chatton, *Current Diagnosis and Treatment* (California: Lange Medical Publications, 1973).

Chapter 7

1. Alfred M. Freedman and Harold I. Kaplan, *Comprehensive Testbook.*

2. Silvano Arieti et al., eds., *American Handbook of Psychiatry,* 2nd ed. (New York: Basic Books, Inc., 1974).

3. Merril Eaton and Margaret Peterson, *Psychiatry.*

4. Lawrence C. Kolb, *Modern Clinical Psychiatry* (Philadelphia: W. B. Saunders Company, 1973).

5. Solomon and Patch, *Handbook.*

6. Shannon and Backus, "Depression," *The Journal of the Arkansas Medical Society,* July 1973.

7. S. Arieti et al., eds., *American Handbook of Psychiatry.*

8. Shannon and Backus, "Depression."

9. Ibid.

10. Sir Denis Hill and Lee E. Hollister, eds., *Depression* (Wisconsin: Lakeside Laboratories, Inc., 1970).

11. Shannon and Backus, "Depression."

12. Ibid.

13. W. G. Reese, "The Major Cause of Death," *Texas Medicine 66,* September 1970.

14. Solomon and Patch, *Handbook.*

15. Ibid.

16. Bill Gothard, Basic Youth Conflicts.

17. Chuck Singletary, Lecture on the Anatomy of Discouragement (Memphis, 1970).

18. Watchman Nee, *Song of Songs* (Pennsylvania: Christian Literature Crusade, 1965).

19. Chuck Singletary, *Lecture on the Anatomy of Discouragement.*

20. Shannon and Backus, "The Psychodynamics of Depression," *Journal of the Arkansas Medical Society,* Dec., 1973.

21. Ibid.

22. W. K. Zung, "The Pharmacology of Disordered Sleep," *Journal of the American Medical Association* 211: March 2, 1970.

23. William Glasser, *Reality Therapy* (New York: Harper and Row, 1965).

24. Harry Ironside, *Full Assurance* (Chicago: Moody Press).

25. William Glasser, *Reality Therapy.*

Chapter 10

1. Eugene Blueler, *Dementia Praecox or the Group of Schizophrenias* (New York: International Universities, 1966).

2. Jerry Blaylock, "Psychopharmacology," unpublished (University of Arkansas Medical Center, 1972).

3. *Drug Treatment in Psychiatry,* Staff of Central NP Research Laboratory, Veterans Administration Hospital, Perry Point, Maryland (Washington: Veterans Administration).

4. Marcus A. Krupp and Milton J. Chatton, *Current Diagnosis and Treatment.*

5. Robert Shannon, Lecture on Psychodynamics, unpublished (University of Arkansas Medical Center, 1972).

6. Solomon and Patch, *Handbook.*

7. J. R. Smythies, *Biological Psychiatry.*

Chapter 11

1. Thomas A. Harris, *I'm OK—You're OK:* A Practical Guide to TA (New York: Harper and Row, 1969).

2. Kenneth F. Weaver, "The Incredible Universe," *National Geographic* 145 (1974): 589-625.

3. "Seven Minutes With God" (Colorado: Navigators).

4. Glasser, *Reality Therapy.*

Chapter 12

1. Cyrus T. Scofield, "Scofield Notes on Job," *Scofield Reference Bible* (New York: Oxford University Press, 1909).

Index